PYTHON
PROGRAMMING FOR
BEGINNERS

Mastering the Fundamentals
of Python Coding for
Absolute Beginners

RICHARD D. CROWLEY

Table of Contents

This chapter delves into the fundamental building blocks of Python programming: variables, data types, and operators. Understanding these concepts is crucial for writing any meaningful Python code. We'll explore how to store information using variables, learn about the different types of data Python can handle, and discover how operators allow us to manipulate that data.

Type conversion, also known as type casting, is the process of changing a value from one data type to another.1 This is a crucial skill in programming, as you'll often encounter situations where you need to work with data in a specific format. Python provides several built-in functions for type conversion:2

This chapter introduces you to two fundamental data structures in Python: lists and tuples. These collections allow you to store and organize multiple items under a single variable, providing a structured way to manage data. Understanding the nuances of lists and tuples, their similarities, and their differences, is crucial for effective Python

CHAPTER 6   107

Sets are another fundamental data structure in Python, characterized by two key properties: they are unordered and contain only unique elements. "Unordered" means that the elements in a set do not have a specific order; you cannot access them by index. "Unique" means that a set cannot contain duplicate values; if you try to add a duplicate, it will simply be ignored. Sets are defined by enclosing elements in curly braces {}, separated by commas. However, an empty set is created using the set() function, not {} (as this creates an empty dictionary).

CHAPTER 7

Functions: Organizing Your Code Functions are a fundamental building block in programming, acting as self-contained blocks of code designed to perform specific tasks. They are essential for organizing your code, making it more modular, reusable, and easier to understand. This chapter delves into the intricacies of defining functions, working with arguments and parameters, and utilizing return values effectively.

Writing error-free code is a challenging but essential aspect of programming. Errors are inevitable, but knowing how to handle them gracefully and debug your code effectively is what separates a novice programmer from a proficient one. This chapter delves into the different types of errors you'll encounter in Python, introduces exception handling mechanisms, and explores debugging techniques to help you write robust and reliable code.   177

While Python provides built-in exceptions for common errors, you can also create and raise your own custom exceptions.1 This is particularly useful when you want to signal specific error conditions within your code or create more descriptive error messages.2   183

Object-Oriented Programming (OOP) Fundamentals Object-Oriented Programming (OOP) is a programming paradigm that organizes software design around "objects," which are instances of1 "classes."2 OOP offers a powerful and intuitive way to structure code, making it more modular, reusable, and easier to maintain.3 This chapter introduces the fundamental concepts of OOP, focusing on classes and objects, and how to define them in Python.

In Python, you define a class using the class keyword, followed by the class name (using CamelCase convention) and a colon :. The class body contains the definitions of the attributes and methods.

Creating an object, also known as instantiation, is the process of bringing a class to life.1 It's like using the cookie cutter (the class) to make an actual cookie (the object). In Python, you create an object by calling the class name as if it were a function.2 This call invokes the class's constructor (__init__ method), which initializes the object's attributes.

CHAPTER 1

Welcome to the World of Python
1.1 What is Python?

This chapter is your gateway into the captivating realm of Python programming. We'll demystify what Python is, explore the compelling reasons behind its widespread adoption, and guide you through the process of setting up your very own Python development environment. By the end of this chapter, you'll be primed to write and execute your inaugural Python program!

1.2 Why Learn Python?

Python is a high-level, interpreted, general-purpose programming language. Let's dissect this definition piece by piece:

- **High-level:** Unlike low-level languages like assembly, which interact directly with a computer's hardware, Python uses syntax that's closer to human language. This abstraction simplifies the coding process, allowing you to focus on the logic of your program rather than the intricacies of memory management or hardware interaction.
- **Interpreted:** Python code is executed line by line by an interpreter. This contrasts with compiled languages, which require the entire program to be translated into machine code before execution. The interpreted nature of Python facilitates faster development cycles, as you can test and debug code incrementally without the need for a separate compilation step.
- **General-purpose:** Python's versatility shines through in its ability to be applied across a broad spectrum

of domains. From web development and data science to machine learning, scripting, automation, and even game development, Python's adaptability makes it a powerful tool in any programmer's arsenal.

- **Dynamically Typed:** Python is dynamically typed, meaning you don't have to explicitly declare the data type of a variable. The interpreter infers the type[1] at runtime, making the code more concise and readable. This feature contributes to Python's reputation for rapid prototyping and development.

Python was conceived by Guido van Rossum and first released in 1991. Van Rossum's vision for Python was to create a language that emphasized code readability and elegance. This philosophy is encapsulated in the "Zen of Python," a collection of guiding principles that promote clean and uncluttered syntax. You can discover these principles for yourself by typing import this in a Python interpreter.

1.2 Why Learn Python?

Python's popularity has soared in recent years, and its rise is no accident. Here are some compelling reasons to embark on your Python learning journey:

- **Beginner-Friendly:** Python's clear and intuitive syntax makes it an ideal starting point for aspiring programmers. It's often the language of choice in introductory programming courses, providing a gentle introduction to fundamental programming concepts.
- **Thriving Community:** Python boasts a vast and active community of developers. This translates to a wealth of online resources, including tutorials, comprehensive

documentation, active forums, and a plethora of open-source libraries. If you encounter a challenge, chances are someone has already tackled it and shared their solution.

- **Unparalleled Versatility:** As previously mentioned, Python's versatility is a major asset. Whether your interests lie in web development, data analysis, machine learning, or any other area of computing, Python provides the tools and libraries you need to succeed.

- **High Demand in the Job Market:** Python skills are highly sought after by employers across various industries. From startups to established tech giants, companies rely on Python for a multitude of tasks. Learning Python can significantly enhance your career prospects and open doors to exciting opportunities.

- **Rich Ecosystem of Libraries and Frameworks:** Python's extensive collection of libraries and frameworks empowers developers to tackle complex tasks with ease. Libraries like NumPy, Pandas, and Scikit-learn are indispensable for data science, while frameworks like Django and Flask are widely used for web development.

- **Cross-Platform Compatibility:** Python code can run seamlessly on various operating systems, including Windows, macOS, and Linux, without requiring significant modifications. This cross-platform compatibility makes Python a highly portable language.

- **Open Source and Free:** Python is open-source, meaning it's free to use, distribute, and modify. This open nature fosters collaboration and innovation within the Python community.

1.3 Setting Up Your Python Environment

Before you can begin writing Python code, you need to establish your development environment. This involves installing Python and selecting a suitable code editor.

1.3.1 Installing Python

1. **Visit the Official Python Website:** Navigate to the official Python website: https://www.python.org/
2. **Download the Installer:** Go to the "Downloads" section and select the appropriate installer for your operating system (Windows, macOS, or Linux). It's crucial to download the latest stable version of Python 3, as Python 2 is now largely deprecated.
3. **Run the Installer (Windows):** When running the installer on Windows, be sure to check the box

that says "Add Python to PATH." This crucial step ensures that you can run Python from the command line.

4. **Run the Installer (macOS/Linux):** The installation process on macOS and Linux might vary slightly depending on your specific distribution. Consult the documentation for your operating system for detailed instructions. Often, Python 3 is already included, but you might need to install additional packages or set up a virtual environment.

5. **Verify the Installation:** Open a command prompt or terminal window. Type python --version (or python3 --version on some systems) and press Enter. If Python is installed correctly, you should see the version number displayed. This confirms that Python is accessible from your command line. If you encounter an error, double-check your installation

and ensure that Python is added to your system's PATH environment variable (especially on Windows).

After successfully installing Python, you're ready to choose a code editor, which we'll discuss in the next section. This combination of Python and a good code editor will empower you to write and run Python programs effectively.

1.3.2 Choosing a Code Editor (IDLE, VS Code, PyCharm, etc.)

Having installed Python, the next step is to equip yourself with a code editor. While you *could* technically write Python code in a plain text editor like Notepad, a dedicated code editor (or an Integrated Development Environment - IDE) offers a wealth of features that significantly enhance the coding experience. These features not only boost productivity but also aid in error detection and code comprehension.[1]

Here's a breakdown of some popular choices:

- **IDLE (Integrated Development and Learning Environment):** IDLE comes bundled with Python and is a great starting point for beginners.[2] It provides a basic editor with syntax highlighting and a shell for running Python code.[3] While IDLE is simple and easy to learn, it lacks some of the more advanced features found in other editors.[4] Think of it as a starter bicycle – perfect for learning the basics, but you might want something more robust for longer journeys.
- **Visual Studio Code (VS Code):** VS Code, developed by Microsoft, has become a favorite among developers across various languages, including Python.[5] It's a free, lightweight, and highly customizable editor with excellent Python support.[6] VS Code's IntelliSense feature provides

intelligent code completion, helping you write code faster and with fewer errors.[7] It also integrates seamlessly with debugging tools and Git, making it a powerful choice for both beginners and experienced programmers.[8] VS Code's extensibility through plugins allows you to tailor it to your specific needs.[9]

- **PyCharm:** PyCharm is a dedicated Python IDE developed by JetBrains.[10] It's a more feature-rich and robust option compared to VS Code, offering advanced features like code refactoring, static analysis, and integrated testing tools. PyCharm is available in two editions: a free Community Edition, which is perfect for learning and small projects, and a paid Professional Edition, which offers more advanced features for professional development.[11] PyCharm's comprehensive nature can be a bit overwhelming for absolute beginners, but it's an excellent choice for those looking for a powerful and integrated development environment.

- **Sublime Text:** Sublime Text is a sophisticated text editor known for its speed and customizability.[12] While not specifically designed for Python, it offers excellent Python support through plugins. Sublime Text is a paid editor, but it offers a free trial.[13] It's a good option for developers who appreciate a lightweight and highly configurable editor.

- **Atom:** Atom, developed by GitHub, is another free and open-source code editor that's highly customizable.[14] It offers good Python support through packages and is a solid choice for beginners and experienced developers alike.

Recommendation: For beginners, VS Code or PyCharm Community Edition are excellent choices. VS Code offers a good balance of features and ease of use, while PyCharm provides a more comprehensive environment. IDLE is also a perfectly acceptable starting point, especially if you're completely new to programming. Don't get too hung up on choosing the "perfect" editor right away. You can always switch later if you find that your needs change.

1.3.3 Running Your First Python Program ("Hello, World!")

With Python installed and a code editor chosen, you're ready to write your first Python program! The classic "Hello, World!" program is a rite of passage for every new programmer. It's a simple program that prints the text "Hello, World!" to the console, but it serves as a crucial test of your setup.

Here's how to create and run your "Hello, World!" program:

1. **Open your code editor:** Launch your chosen code editor (VS Code, PyCharm, IDLE, etc.).
2. **Create a new file:** Create a new file and save it with a .py extension. For example, hello.py. The .py extension tells your operating system that this is a Python file.
3. **Write the code:** In the hello.py file, type the following line of code:
4. Python

```python
print("Hello, World!")
```

5.
6. This line uses the print() function, a built-in Python function that displays output to the console. The text you want to print is enclosed in double quotes.
7. **Save the file:** Save the hello.py file.
8. **Run the code:**

- From the command line/terminal: Open your command prompt or terminal. Navigate to the directory where you saved hello.py. Then, type python hello.py (or python3 hello.py depending on your system) and press Enter.
- **From your code editor:** Most code editors have a "Run" button or a keyboard shortcut to execute Python code directly. Consult your editor's documentation for specific instructions.

9. **Observe the output:** If everything is configured correctly, you should see "Hello, World!" printed in your console or the editor's output window.

Congratulations! You've just written and run your first Python program!

1.4 Python's Strengths and Applications

Python's widespread popularity stems from its numerous strengths:

- **Readability:** Python's syntax is designed for clarity, making code easier to read, write, and maintain.[15]
- **Extensive Libraries:** Python's vast standard library and the availability of numerous third-party libraries cater to a wide range of tasks, from web development to data science.[16]
- **Cross-Platform Compatibility:** Python code can run on various operating systems without significant modifications.[17]
- **Large and Active Community:** Python's large community provides ample support and resources for learners and developers.[18]

- **Open Source:** Python's open-source nature fosters collaboration and innovation.

These strengths make Python suitable for a diverse range of applications:

- **Web Development:** Frameworks like Django and Flask empower developers to build robust web applications.[19]
- **Data Science and Machine Learning:** Libraries like NumPy, Pandas, Scikit-learn, and TensorFlow make Python the language of choice for data analysis and machine learning.[20]
- **Scripting and Automation:** Python excels at automating repetitive tasks and scripting system administration.[21]
- **Game Development:** While not as prevalent as C++, Python is used in

game development, especially for scripting and prototyping.[22]

- **Desktop GUI Development:** Libraries like Tkinter, PyQt, and Kivy enable the creation of desktop applications with graphical interfaces.[23]

1.5 Introduction to Programming Concepts

Programming involves creating a set of instructions that tell a computer what to do. Here are some fundamental programming concepts:

- **Variables:** Variables store data.[24] They are like containers that hold values.
- **Data Types:** Data types classify the kind of data a variable can hold (e.g., integers, floats, strings, booleans).

- **Operators:** Operators perform operations on data (e.g., arithmetic operators, comparison operators, logical operators).[25]
- **Control Flow:** Control flow statements dictate the order in which instructions are executed (e.g., conditional statements, loops).[26]
- **Functions:** Functions are reusable blocks of code that perform specific tasks.[27]
- **Data Structures:** Data structures organize and store data (e.g., lists, tuples, dictionaries).[28]
- **Algorithms:** Algorithms are step-by-step instructions for solving a problem.[29]
- **Object-Oriented Programming (OOP):** OOP is a programming paradigm that organizes code around "objects," which are instances of classes.[30]

These concepts will be explored in detail throughout this book. Remember, practice is key to mastering programming. Don't be afraid to experiment and try different things!

CHAPTER 2:

Variables, Data Types, and Operators

This chapter delves into the fundamental building blocks of Python programming: variables, data types, and operators. Understanding these concepts is crucial for writing any meaningful Python code. We'll explore how to store information using variables, learn about the different types of data Python can handle, and discover how operators allow us to manipulate that data.

2.1 Variables: Storing Information

Imagine variables as labeled containers that hold information.[1] They are the cornerstone of any programming language, allowing you to store and manipulate data dynamically.[2]

In Python, creating a variable is remarkably simple: you just assign a value to a name.[3]

Creating Variables:

Python

```
name = "Alice"
age = 30
height = 5.8
is_student = True
```

In this example:

- name is a variable storing the string "Alice".
- age is a variable storing the integer 30.
- height is a variable storing the floating-point number 5.8.
- is_student is a variable storing the boolean value True.

Naming Variables:

Python has specific rules for naming variables:

- Variable names can contain letters (a-z, A-Z), numbers (0-9), and underscores[4] (_).
- The first character cannot be a number.[5]
- Variable names are case-sensitive (e.g., name and Name are different variables).
- It's best practice to use descriptive names that reflect the variable's purpose (e.g., student_name is better than sn).
- Avoid using reserved keywords (like print, if, for) as variable names.

Assigning and Reassigning Values:

You can assign a new value to an existing variable at any time:

Python

```
age = 30  # Initial assignment
print(age)  # Output: 30

age = 31  # Reassignment
print(age)  # Output: 31
```

Multiple Assignments:

Python allows you to assign the same value to multiple variables simultaneously:

Python

```
x = y = z = 10
print(x, y, z)  # Output: 10 10 10
```

You can also assign different values to multiple variables in a single line:

Python

```
a, b, c = 1, 2, 3
print(a, b, c)  # Output: 1 2 3
```

2.2 Data Types: Integers, Floats, Strings, Booleans

Data types classify the kind of information a variable can hold. Python has several built-in data types, including:

- **Integers (int):** Integers represent whole numbers (e.g., -10, 0, 100).[6]

Python

```
count = 150
temperature = -5
```

- **Floats (float):** Floats represent numbers with decimal points (e.g., 3.14, -2.5, 0.0).[7]

Python

```
pi = 3.14159
price = 99.99
```

- **Strings (str):** Strings represent sequences of characters (text). They are enclosed in single quotes (' '), double quotes (" "), or triple quotes (''' or[8] """).

Python

```
message = "Hello, World!"
name = 'Bob'
multiline_string = """This is a
multiline string."""
```

- **Booleans (bool):** Booleans represent truth values: True or False.

They are often used in conditional statements.

Python

```
is_active = True
has_permission = False
```

Determining Data Type:

You can use the type() function to determine the data type of a variable:

Python

```
age = 30
print(type(age))  # Output: <class 'int'>

name = "Alice"
print(type(name))  # Output: <class 'str'>
```

Type Conversion (Casting):

You can convert a value from one data type to another using type casting functions:

Python

```python
age_str = "25"
age_int = int(age_str)  # Convert string to integer
print(type(age_int)) # Output: <class 'int'>

height = 5.7
height_int = int(height)  # Convert float to integer (truncates decimal part)
print(height_int)     # Output: 5

price = 99
price_float = float(price) # Convert int to float
print(price_float)    # Output: 99.0

is_adult = "True"
is_adult_bool = bool(is_adult) # Convert string to boolean
print(is_adult_bool)       # Output: True (most non-empty strings are True)
```

```
is_empty = ""
is_empty_bool = bool(is_empty) # Convert
empty string to boolean
print(is_empty_bool)        # Output: False
(empty strings are False)
```

Understanding variables and data types is fundamental to programming. They allow you to store and manipulate information effectively, forming the basis for more complex operations and program logic.[9] In the next section, we'll explore operators, which enable you to perform actions on these variables and data types.

2.3 Type Conversion

Type conversion, also known as type casting, is the process of changing a value from one data type to another.[1] This is a crucial skill in programming, as you'll often encounter situations where you need to work with data in a specific format. Python provides several built-in functions for type conversion:[2]

- int(): Converts a value to an integer. If the value is a float, the decimal part is truncated (not rounded).[3] If the value is a string, it must represent a valid integer.
- float(): Converts a value to a floating-point number. If the value is an integer, it's converted to a float with a decimal part of .0. If the value is a string, it must represent a valid float.
- str(): Converts a value to a string. Any data type can be converted to a string.[4]

- bool(): Converts a value to a boolean. Most values convert to True, except for empty strings, 0, None, and empty collections (like lists, tuples, and dictionaries).

Examples:

Python

```
age_str = "30"
age_int = int(age_str)  # Convert string to integer
print(age_int, type(age_int))  # Output: 30 <class 'int'>

price = 99.99
price_int = int(price)  # Convert float to integer (truncates decimal part)
print(price_int, type(price_int))  # Output: 99 <class 'int'>

is_active = True
```

```python
is_active_str = str(is_active)   # Convert
boolean to string
print(is_active_str, type(is_active_str))   #
Output: True <class 'str'>

height = 5.7
height_str = str(height) # Convert float to
string
print(height_str,     type(height_str))     #
Output: 5.7 <class 'str'>

zero = 0
zero_bool = bool(zero)
print(zero_bool, type(zero_bool)) # Output:
False <class 'bool'>

one = 1
one_bool = bool(one)
print(one_bool, type(one_bool)) # Output:
True <class 'bool'>

empty_string = ""
empty_string_bool = bool(empty_string)
```

```python
print(empty_string_bool,
type(empty_string_bool))  # Output: False
<class 'bool'>
```

Implicit Type Conversion (Coercion):

In some cases, Python performs implicit type conversion, also known as coercion.[5] This often happens during arithmetic operations:

Python

```python
result = 5 + 3.14   # Python implicitly
converts 5 to a float before adding
print(result, type(result))   # Output: 8.14
<class 'float'>
```

2.4 Operators: Arithmetic, Comparison, Logical, Assignment

Operators are symbols that perform operations on values.[6] Python provides a wide range of operators:

- **Arithmetic Operators:** Used for mathematical calculations:
  - +: Addition
  - -: Subtraction
  - *: Multiplication
  - /: Division (returns a float)
  - //: Floor Division (returns an integer)
  - %: Modulus (remainder)
  - **: Exponentiation
- **Comparison Operators:** Used to compare values:
  - ==: Equal to
  - !=: Not equal to
  - >: Greater than
  - <: Less than

- $\circ$ >=: Greater than or equal to
- $\circ$ <=: Less than or equal[7] to
- **Logical Operators:** Used to combine or modify boolean values:
  - $\circ$ and: Returns True if both operands are True
  - $\circ$ or: Returns True if at least one operand is True
  - $\circ$ not: Returns the opposite of the operand[8]
- **Assignment Operators:** Used to assign values to variables:
  - $\circ$ =: Assignment
  - $\circ$ +=: Add and assign
  - $\circ$ -=: Subtract and assign
  - $\circ$ *=: Multiply and assign
  - $\circ$ /=: Divide and assign
  - $\circ$ //=: Floor divide and assign
  - $\circ$ %=: Modulus and assign
  - $\circ$ **=: Exponentiate and assign[9]

Examples:

Python

```python
x = 10
y = 3

print(x + y)  # Output: 13
print(x / y)  # Output: 3.3333333333333335
print(x // y) # Output: 3
print(x % y)  # Output: 1
print(x ** y) # Output: 1000

print(x > y)  # Output: True
print(x == y) # Output: False

a = True
b = False
print(a and b)  # Output: False
print(a or b)   # Output: True
print(not a)    # Output: False

x += 5  # Equivalent to x = x + 5
print(x)  # Output: 15
```

2.5 Operator Precedence

Operator precedence determines the order in which operations are performed in an expression.[10] Python follows standard mathematical precedence rules:[11]

1. Parentheses (): Operations inside parentheses are performed first.
2. Exponentiation **: Exponentiation is performed next.
3. Multiplication, Division, Floor Division, Modulus *, /, //, %: These are performed from left to right.
4. Addition, Subtraction +, -: These are performed from left to right.
5. Comparison operators, Logical operators are evaluated after arithmetic operations.

You can use parentheses to override the default precedence:

Python

```
result = 2 + 3 * 4   # Multiplication is
performed before addition
print(result) # Output: 14

result = (2 + 3) * 4   # Parentheses force
addition to be performed first
print(result) # Output: 20
```

2.6 Working with Strings: Concatenation, Formatting

Strings are a fundamental data type in Python, and there are several ways to manipulate them:

- **Concatenation:** You can combine strings using the + operator:

Python

```
greeting = "Hello"
name = "Alice"
message = greeting + ", " + name + "!"
print(message)  # Output: Hello, Alice!
```

- **String Formatting:** String formatting allows you to create strings with embedded values.[12] There are several ways to do this:
  - **f-strings (Formatted String Literals):** f-strings are the most modern and convenient way to format strings.[13] You can embed expressions inside curly braces {} within the string:
- Python

```
name = "Bob"
age = 25
```

```
print(f"My name is {name} and I am {age}
years old.")  # Output: My name is Bob and
I am 25 years old.
```

-

  - str.format() **method:** You can
    use the format() method to
    replace placeholders in a string
    with values:
- Python

```
name = "Charlie"
score = 100
print("Name: {}, Score: {}".format(name,
score))  # Output: Name: Charlie, Score:
100
print("Name: {0}, Score: {1}".format(name,
score))  # Output: Name: Charlie, Score:
100 (explicit indexing)
print("Name:          {name},          Score:
{score}".format(name=name, score=score))
```

```python
# Output: Name: Charlie, Score: 100
(keyword arguments)
```

-
  - % **operator (Old style formatting):** This is an older style of formatting that is still supported but less preferred than f-strings or str.format():
- Python

```python
name = "David"
percentage = 95.5
print("Name: %s, Percentage: %.2f" % (name, percentage))  # Output: Name: David, Percentage: 95.50
```

-
-

String formatting is essential for creating clear and informative output, especially when dealing with variables and dynamic data.[14] F-strings are generally recommended for their readability and ease of use.

CHAPTER 3

Control Flow: Making Decisions

This chapter explores the crucial concept of control flow in Python, specifically focusing on how to make decisions within your programs. Control flow determines the order in which statements are executed, and conditional statements are the tools that allow your programs to respond dynamically to different situations. We'll delve into `if`, `elif`, and `else` statements, explore nested conditionals, understand boolean expressions and truth tables, and work through practical examples to solidify your understanding.

3.1 Conditional Statements: if, elif, else

Conditional statements are the foundation of decision-making in programming. They allow your code to execute different blocks of instructions based on whether a specific condition is true or false. Python provides three primary keywords for conditional statements: `if`, `elif` (else if), and `else`.

* **`if` statement:** The `if` statement executes a block of code only if a condition is true.

```python
if condition:
    # Code to execute if the condition is true
```

* **`elif` statement:** The `elif` statement is used when you have multiple conditions to check. It's executed if the preceding `if` condition is false, but the

`elif` condition is true. You can have multiple `elif` statements.

```python
if condition1:
    # Code to execute if condition1 is true
elif condition2:
    # Code to execute if condition1 is false and
condition2 is true
```

* **`else` statement:** The `else` statement is executed if none of the preceding `if` or `elif` conditions are true. It provides a default case.

```python
if condition1:
    # Code to execute if condition1 is true
elif condition2:
    # Code to execute if condition1 is false and
condition2 is true
else:
```

```
    # Code to execute if neither condition1
nor condition2 is true
```

Example:

```python
age = 20

if age < 18:
    print("You are a minor.")
elif age >= 18 and age < 65:
    print("You are an adult.")
else:
    print("You are a senior citizen.")
```

In this example, the code first checks if
`age` is less than 18. If it is, the first `print`
statement is executed. Otherwise, it checks
if `age` is greater than or equal to 18 *and*
less than 65. If this is true, the second
`print` statement is executed. Finally, if
neither of these conditions is true (meaning

`age` is 65 or older), the `else` block is executed.

3.2 Nested Conditional Statements

Nested conditional statements occur when you place an `if`, `elif`, or `else` statement *inside* another conditional statement. This allows you to create more complex decision-making logic.

```python
temperature = 25
is_raining = False

if temperature > 20:
    print("It's warm.")
    if not is_raining:
        print("And it's sunny!")
    else:
        print("But it's raining.")
else:
    print("It's cool.")
```

```

```

In this example, the outer `if` statement checks if the temperature is greater than 20. If it is, the inner `if` statement checks if it's raining. This nested structure allows for more specific responses based on multiple factors.

3.3 Boolean Expressions and Truth Tables

Boolean expressions are expressions that evaluate to either `True` or `False`. They are the core of conditional statements. Boolean expressions often involve comparison operators (e.g., `==`, `!=`, `>`, `<`) and logical operators (e.g., `and`, `or`, `not`).

Truth tables are a way to visualize the results of logical operations. Here are the truth tables for the three main logical operators:

* **`and`:**

Operand 1	Operand 2	Result
True	True	True
True	False	False
False	True	False
False	False	False

* **`or`:**

Operand 1	Operand 2	Result
True	True	True
True	False	True
False	True	True
False	False	False

* **`not`:**

Operand	Result
True	False

| False | True |

Understanding truth tables is essential for writing correct and effective boolean expressions.

3.4 Practical Examples: Building Simple Decision-Making Programs

Let's work through some practical examples to illustrate the use of conditional statements:

Example 1: A Simple Grade Calculator

```python
score = 85

if score >= 90:
    grade = "A"
elif score >= 80:
    grade = "B"
elif score >= 70:
```

```python
    grade = "C"
elif score >= 60:
    grade = "D"
else:
    grade = "F"

print(f"Your grade is {grade}.")
```

Example 2: Checking for Even or Odd

```python
number = 17

if number % 2 == 0:
    print(f"{number} is even.")
else:
    print(f"{number} is odd.")
```

Example 3: A Simple Traffic Light Simulation

```python
```

```python
light_color = "red"

if light_color == "green":
    print("Go!")
elif light_color == "yellow":
    print("Caution!")
elif light_color == "red":
    print("Stop!")
else:
    print("Invalid light color.")
```

These examples demonstrate how conditional statements can be used to create programs that make decisions based on different conditions. By combining `if`, `elif`, and `else` statements with boolean expressions, you can build complex logic into your Python programs. Practice writing your own decision-making programs to solidify your understanding of this important concept.

CHAPTER 4

Loops: Repeating Actions

In programming, loops are essential tools that allow you to automate repetitive tasks.[1] Instead of writing the same code multiple times, you can use a loop to execute a block of code repeatedly.[2] This not only saves you time and effort but also makes your code more concise and easier to maintain.[3] Python provides two primary types of loops: for loops and while loops. Each serves a slightly different purpose, and understanding their nuances is key to writing efficient and effective code.

4.1 for Loops: Iterating over Sequences

for loops are specifically designed for iterating over sequences, such as lists, tuples, strings, and ranges. They execute a block of code once for each item in the sequence.[4] The basic syntax of a for loop is:

Python

```
for item in sequence:
    # Code to execute for each item
```

- item: This variable represents the current item being processed in the sequence. It takes on the value of each item in the sequence in turn.[5]
- sequence: This is the sequence you want to iterate over. It can be a list, tuple, string, or any other iterable object.[6]

Examples:

- **Iterating over a list:**

Python

```python
fruits = ["apple", "banana", "cherry"]

for fruit in fruits:
    print(fruit)
```

Output:

```
apple
banana
cherry
```

- **Iterating over a string:**

Python

```python
message = "Hello"

for char in message:
    print(char)
```

Output:

```
H
e
l
l
o
```

- **Iterating over a range:**

The range() function generates a sequence of numbers. You can use it with a for loop to repeat a block of code a specific number of times.

Python

```
for i in range(5):  # Generates numbers from
0 to 4
    print(i)
```

Output:

```
0
1
2
3
4
```

You can also specify a start and end value for the range() function:

Python

```
for i in range(2, 7):  # Generates numbers
from 2 to 6
    print(i)
```

Output:

```
2
3
4
5
```

6

And you can even specify a step value:

Python

```python
for i in range(0, 10, 2):  # Generates even numbers from 0 to 8
    print(i)
```

Output:

```
0
2
4
6
8
```

4.2 while Loops: Repeating Until a Condition is Met

while loops are used when you want to repeat a block of code as long as a certain condition is true. The loop continues to execute until the condition becomes false. The basic syntax of a while loop is:

Python

```
while condition:
    # Code to execute while the condition is
true
```

It's crucial to ensure that the condition eventually becomes false; otherwise, you'll create an infinite loop, which will run indefinitely.

Examples:

- **Counting loop:**

Python

```
count = 0

while count < 5:
    print(count)
    count += 1  # Increment count to avoid an infinite loop
```

Output:

```
0
1
2
3
4
```

- **Looping until a user input is valid:**

Python

```python
while True:
    age = input("Enter your age: ")
    if age.isdigit() and int(age) > 0:
        break  # Exit the loop if the input is valid
    else:
        print("Invalid age. Please enter a positive integer.")

age = int(age) # since the age is string, we have to convert it to int after the loop is over.
print(f"Your age is {age}.")
```

In this example, the loop continues to prompt the user for their age until they enter a valid positive integer. The break statement is used to exit the loop once the condition is met.

Choosing between for and while loops:

- Use a for loop when you know the number of iterations in advance (e.g., iterating over a sequence).
- Use a while loop when the number of iterations is unknown and depends on a condition (e.g., looping until a user provides valid input).

Loop Control Statements:

Python provides several loop control statements that allow you to modify the behavior of loops:[8]

- break:[9] Exits the loop immediately.
- continue: Skips the current iteration and proceeds to the next iteration.
- pass: Does nothing. It's often used as a placeholder when you need a statement syntactically but don't want to execute any code.

These loop control statements offer finer-grained control over how your loops operate, allowing you to create more sophisticated and efficient code. Understanding when and how to use them is a valuable skill in programming.

4.3 Loop Control Statements: break, continue, pass

Loop control statements provide fine-grained control over the execution of loops. They allow you to alter the normal flow of a loop, either by exiting the loop prematurely or skipping certain iterations. Python offers three primary loop control statements: break, continue, and pass.

- break: The break statement immediately terminates the loop, regardless of whether the loop condition is still true. When a break statement is encountered, the program execution jumps to the statement following the loop. break is often used when a specific condition is met, and there's no need to continue iterating.

Python

```python
for i in range(10):
    if i == 5:
        break  # Exit the loop when i reaches 5
    print(i)
```

Output:

```
0
1
2
3
4
```

- continue: The continue statement skips the remaining statements in the current iteration of the loop and proceeds to the next iteration. It's useful when you want to bypass certain iterations based on a condition but still want the loop to continue executing.

Python

```python
for i in range(10):
    if i % 2 == 0:  # Skip even numbers
        continue
    print(i)
```

Output:

```
1
3
5
7
9
```

- pass: The pass statement does nothing. It's a null operation. It's often used as a placeholder when you need a statement syntactically but don't want to execute any code. This can be useful when you're still developing your code or when you need an empty block in a conditional statement or a loop.

Python

```python
for i in range(5):
    if i == 2:
        pass  # Do nothing when i is 2
    else:
        print(i)
```

Output:

```
0
1
```

3

4

4.4 Nested Loops

Nested loops occur when you place one loop inside another loop. The inner loop executes completely for each iteration of the outer loop. Nested loops are useful for iterating over multidimensional data structures or for performing tasks that require multiple levels of iteration.

Python

```python
for i in range(3):  # Outer loop
    for j in range(2):  # Inner loop
        print(f"i: {i}, j: {j}")
```

Output:

i: 0, j: 0
i: 0, j: 1
i: 1, j: 0
i: 1, j: 1
i: 2, j: 0
i: 2, j: 1

In this example, the outer loop iterates three times, and for each iteration of the outer loop, the inner loop iterates twice.

Example: Printing a multiplication table:

Python

```
for i in range(1, 11):
    for j in range(1, 11):
        print(f"{i} * {j} = {i*j}", end="\t")  # end="\t" adds a tab instead of a newline
    print()  # Print a newline after each row
```

This code will print a multiplication table from 1 to 10.

4.5 Practical Examples: Automating Repetitive Tasks

Loops are incredibly useful for automating repetitive tasks. Here are some practical examples:

- **Processing a list of files:**

Python

```
import os

files = os.listdir("my_directory")  # Get a list of files in a directory

for file in files:
    if file.endswith(".txt"):  # Process only text files
        with open(os.path.join("my_directory", file), "r") as f:
```

```python
    # Read and process the contents of the file
    content = f.read()
    # ... process content ...
```

- **Generating reports:**

Python

```python
data = [
    {"name": "Alice", "score": 90},
    {"name": "Bob", "score": 85},
    {"name": "Charlie", "score": 95},
]

for item in data:
    print(f'Name: {item['name']}, Score: {item['score']}")
```

- **Web scraping:**

Python

```python
import requests
from bs4 import BeautifulSoup

url = "https://www.example.com"
response = requests.get(url)
soup = BeautifulSoup(response.content, "html.parser")

for link in soup.find_all("a"):
    href = link.get("href")
    if href:
        print(href)
```

These examples demonstrate how loops can be used to automate a wide range of tasks, from file processing and report generation to web scraping and data analysis. By mastering loops and loop control statements, you can significantly increase your productivity and write more efficient and effective code. Remember to consider whether a for or while loop is more appropriate for your specific task and to use loop control statements judiciously to achieve the desired behavior. Practice automating different tasks with loops to solidify your understanding and unlock the true power of repetitive execution in programming.

CHAPTER 5:

Working with Collections: Lists and Tuples

This chapter introduces you to two fundamental data structures in Python: lists and tuples. These collections allow you to store and organize multiple items under a single variable, providing a structured way to manage data. Understanding the nuances of lists and tuples, their similarities, and their differences, is crucial for effective Python programming.

5.1 Lists: Creating, Accessing, and Modifying

Lists are ordered, mutable sequences of items. "Ordered" means that the items in a list maintain a specific order, and "mutable" means that you can change the contents of a list after it's created. Lists are defined by enclosing items in square brackets [], separated by commas.

Creating Lists:

Python

```
fruits = ["apple", "banana", "cherry"]  # List of strings
numbers = [1, 2, 3, 4, 5]  # List of integers
mixed_list = [1, "hello", 3.14, True]  # List of mixed data types
empty_list = []  # Empty list
```

Accessing List Elements:

You can access individual elements in a list using indexing. List indices start at 0 for the first element, 1 for the second element, and so on.

Python

```
fruits = ["apple", "banana", "cherry"]
```

```
print(fruits[0])  # Output: apple
print(fruits[1])  # Output: banana
print(fruits[2])  # Output: cherry

print(fruits[-1]) # Output: cherry (Accessing
the last element using negative index)
print(fruits[-2])    #    Output:    banana
(Accessing the second to last element using
negative index)
```

Modifying Lists:

Lists are mutable, which means you can change their contents after they're created.

- **Changing an element:**

Python

```
fruits[0] = "grape"
print(fruits)   # Output: ['grape', 'banana',
'cherry']
```

- **Adding elements:** (covered in more detail in the next section)
- **Removing elements:** (covered in more detail in the next section)
- **Slicing:** You can extract a portion of a list using slicing:

Python

```python
numbers = [1, 2, 3, 4, 5]

print(numbers[1:4])   # Output: [2, 3, 4]
(elements from index 1 up to, but not
including, index 4)
print(numbers[:3])    # Output: [1, 2, 3]
(elements from the beginning up to, but not
including, index 3)
print(numbers[2:])    # Output: [3, 4, 5]
(elements from index 2 to the end)
print(numbers[:])   # Output: [1, 2, 3, 4, 5]
(A copy of the entire list)
```

```python
print(numbers[1:4:2])  # Output: [2, 4]
```
(Elements from index 1 up to, but not including, index 4 with a step of 2)

5.2 List Operations: Appending, Inserting, Removing, Sorting

Python provides a variety of built-in functions and methods for manipulating lists.

- **Appending:** The append() method adds an element to the end of the list.

Python

```python
fruits = ["apple", "banana"]
fruits.append("orange")
print(fruits)  # Output: ['apple', 'banana', 'orange']
```

- **Inserting:** The insert() method inserts an element at a specific index.

Python

```python
fruits = ["apple", "banana"]
fruits.insert(1, "grape")  # Insert "grape" at index 1
print(fruits)   # Output: ['apple', 'grape', 'banana']
```

- **Extending:** The extend() method adds all elements of an iterable (like another list) to the end of the list.

Python

```python
fruits = ["apple", "banana"]
more_fruits = ["orange", "mango"]
fruits.extend(more_fruits)
```

```python
print(fruits)   # Output: ['apple', 'banana', 'orange', 'mango']
```

- **Removing:**
  - remove(): Removes the first occurrence of a specific value.
- Python

```python
fruits = ["apple", "banana", "apple"]
fruits.remove("apple")
print(fruits)  # Output: ['banana', 'apple']
```

-
  - pop(): Removes and returns the element at a specific index.
- Python

```python
fruits = ["apple", "banana", "cherry"]
```

```
removed_fruit = fruits.pop(1)   # Remove
and return the element at index 1
print(fruits) # Output: ['apple', 'cherry']
print(removed_fruit) # Output: banana
```

-
- If no index is given to pop(), it removes and returns the last element of the list.
  - clear(): Removes all items from the list.
- Python

```
fruits = ["apple", "banana", "cherry"]
fruits.clear()
print(fruits) # Output: []
```

-
-
- **Sorting:**

- sort(): Sorts the list in place (modifies the original list). By default, it sorts in ascending order.
- Python

```python
numbers = [3, 1, 4, 2]
numbers.sort()
print(numbers)  # Output: [1, 2, 3, 4]

fruits = ["banana", "apple", "cherry"]
fruits.sort()
print(fruits)  # Output: ['apple', 'banana', 'cherry']
```

-
- You can sort in descending order by passing reverse=True as an argument to the sort() method.
- Python

```
numbers = [3, 1, 4, 2]
numbers.sort(reverse=True)
print(numbers)  # Output: [4, 3, 2, 1]
```

-

  - o sorted(): Returns a new sorted list without modifying the original list.
- Python

```
numbers = [3, 1, 4, 2]
sorted_numbers = sorted(numbers)
print(numbers)       # Output: [3, 1, 4, 2]
(original list unchanged)
print(sorted_numbers) # Output: [1, 2, 3, 4]
(new sorted list)
```

-
-
- **Other Useful List Methods:**

- count(): Returns the number of times a specific value appears in the list.
- Python

```python
numbers = [1, 2, 2, 3, 2]
count = numbers.count(2)
print(count)  # Output: 3
```

-

  - index(): Returns the index of the first occurrence of a specific value.
- Python

```python
fruits = ["apple", "banana", "cherry"]
index = fruits.index("banana")
print(index)  # Output: 1
```

-

- ○ reverse(): Reverses the order of the elements in the list in place.
- Python

```
numbers = [1, 2, 3, 4]
numbers.reverse()
print(numbers)  # Output: [4, 3, 2, 1]
```

-
-

Understanding and utilizing these list operations is crucial for effectively managing and manipulating data within your Python programs. Lists are versatile and widely used, so mastering them is a fundamental step in your Python learning journey.

5.3 Tuples: Immutable Sequences

Tuples are another type of sequence in Python, similar to lists but with one crucial difference: they are *immutable*. This means that once a tuple is created, its contents cannot be changed.[1] Tuples are defined by enclosing items in parentheses (), separated by commas. While parentheses are optional in some cases, it is best practice to always include them for clarity and consistency.

Creating Tuples:

Python

```
fruits = ("apple", "banana", "cherry")   # Tuple of strings
numbers = (1, 2, 3, 4, 5) # Tuple of integers
mixed_tuple = (1, "hello", 3.14, True)   # Tuple of mixed data types
empty_tuple = ()  # Empty tuple
```

one_element_tuple = (5,) # Tuple with single element. The trailing comma is important.

Accessing Tuple Elements:

Just like lists, you can access individual elements in a tuple using indexing, starting from 0.[2]

Python

```
fruits = ("apple", "banana", "cherry")

print(fruits[0])  # Output: apple
print(fruits[1])  # Output: banana
print(fruits[2])  # Output: cherry
print(fruits[-1]) # Output: cherry
```

Immutability:

The key difference between lists and tuples is that tuples are immutable.[3] You cannot change the elements of a tuple after it's created.[4] Attempting to modify a tuple will result in an error.[5]

Python

```
fruits = ("apple", "banana", "cherry")
# fruits[0] = "grape"   # This will raise a
TypeError: 'tuple' object does not support
item assignment
```

Why Immutability?

While it might seem like a limitation, immutability offers several advantages:

- **Data Integrity:** Immutability ensures that the data in a tuple remains constant throughout the program's execution.[6] This can be crucial when representing data that should not be changed, such as coordinates or database records.

- **Performance:** Tuples are often slightly more memory-efficient and faster to process than lists due to their immutability.[7]
- **Use as Dictionary Keys:** Because tuples are immutable, they can be used as keys in dictionaries, whereas lists cannot.

5.4 Tuple Operations

Although you cannot modify the elements of a tuple, you can still perform some operations on them:

- **Concatenation:** You can concatenate tuples using the + operator. This creates a *new* tuple containing the elements of both original tuples.

Python

```
tuple1 = (1, 2, 3)
tuple2 = (4, 5, 6)
combined_tuple = tuple1 + tuple2
print(combined_tuple)  # Output: (1, 2, 3, 4,
5, 6)
```

- **Slicing:** Slicing works the same way as with lists, returning a *new* tuple containing the specified portion of the original tuple.

Python

```
numbers = (1, 2, 3, 4, 5)

print(numbers[1:4])  # Output: (2, 3, 4)
```

- **Other Operations:** Many of the operations that don't modify the tuple (like len(), count(), and index()) work the same way as with lists.

Python

```python
fruits = ("apple", "banana", "cherry", "apple")
print(len(fruits))      # Output: 4
print(fruits.count("apple")) # Output: 2
print(fruits.index("banana")) # Output: 1
```

5.5   List   Comprehensions (Introduction)

List comprehensions provide a concise and elegant way to create new lists based on existing iterables (like lists, tuples, or ranges). They offer a more compact syntax compared to traditional for loops for list creation.

Basic Syntax:

Python

new_list = [expression for item in iterable if condition]

- expression: The value to be included in the new list.
- item: The variable representing each[8] item in the iterable.
- iterable: The sequence to iterate over.
- condition (optional): A filter that determines which items to include.

Examples:

- **Creating a list of squares:**

Python

```
numbers = [1, 2, 3, 4, 5]
squares = [x**2 for x in numbers]
print(squares)  # Output: [1, 4, 9, 16, 25]
```

- **Filtering even numbers:**

Python

```python
numbers = [1, 2, 3, 4, 5, 6]
even_numbers = [x for x in numbers if x % 2 == 0]
print(even_numbers)  # Output: [2, 4, 6]
```

- **Converting strings to uppercase:**

Python

```python
fruits = ["apple", "banana", "cherry"]
uppercase_fruits = [fruit.upper() for fruit in fruits]
print(uppercase_fruits)  # Output: ['APPLE', 'BANANA', 'CHERRY']
```

List comprehensions are a powerful tool for creating and manipulating lists efficiently.[9] They can often replace multiple lines of code with a single, concise expression. While we've only introduced the basics here, list comprehensions can be more complex and versatile, including nested loops and conditional expressions. We will explore them in more detail in a later chapter.

CHAPTER 6

More Collections: Dictionaries and Sets

This chapter expands our exploration of Python collections by introducing two more powerful and versatile data structures: dictionaries and sets. Dictionaries provide a way to store data in key-value pairs, allowing for efficient lookups and organization. Sets, on the other hand, are unordered collections of unique elements, useful for tasks like removing duplicates and performing set operations. Mastering these collections will significantly enhance your ability to work with data in Python.

6.1 Dictionaries: Key-Value Pairs

Dictionaries are unordered collections of key-value pairs. Each key in a dictionary must be unique and immutable (e.g., strings, numbers, or tuples), while the values can be of any data type. Dictionaries are defined by enclosing key-value pairs in curly braces {}, with keys and values separated by a colon : and pairs separated by commas. Think of a dictionary like a real-world dictionary: you look up a "key" (a word), and you find its associated "value" (the definition).

Creating Dictionaries:

Python

```
person = {"name": "Alice", "age": 30, "city": "New York"}   # Dictionary of personal information
inventory = {"apple": 10, "banana": 5, "orange": 20}   # Dictionary representing inventory
empty_dict = {} # Empty dictionary
```

Accessing Dictionary Values:

You can access the value associated with a key using square brackets []:

Python

```python
person = {"name": "Alice", "age": 30, "city": "New York"}

print(person["name"])  # Output: Alice
print(person["age"])  # Output: 30
print(person["city"])  # Output: New York
```

Handling Missing Keys:

Attempting to access a key that doesn't exist in the dictionary will raise a KeyError. To avoid this, you can use the get() method, which allows you to specify a default value to return if the key is not found:

Python

```python
print(person.get("country"))     #  Output: None
```

```
print(person.get("country", "Unknown"))  #
Output: Unknown
```

The get() method is a safer way to access dictionary values, especially when you're not sure if a key exists. It prevents your program from crashing due to a KeyError.

Dictionary Keys:

Dictionary keys must be immutable. This means you can use strings, numbers, or tuples as keys, but you cannot use lists or other mutable objects. Attempting to use a mutable object as a key will result in a TypeError. This restriction is in place because dictionary keys are used for hashing, a process that requires immutability to ensure consistent lookups.

6.2 Dictionary Operations: Adding, Removing, Accessing

Dictionaries provide various methods for adding, removing, and accessing data.

Adding Key-Value Pairs:

- **Direct Assignment:** You can add a new key-value pair to a dictionary by simply assigning a value to a new key:

Python

```
person = {"name": "Alice", "age": 30}
person["country"] = "USA"   # Add a new key-value pair
print(person)   # Output: {'name': 'Alice', 'age': 30, 'country': 'USA'}
```

- update() **Method:** You can also use the update() method to add multiple key-value pairs at once, even merging one dictionary into another:

Python

```
person = {"name": "Alice", "age": 30}
person.update({"country":          "USA",
"occupation": "Software Engineer"})
print(person)   # Output: {'name': 'Alice',
'age':  30,  'country':  'USA',  'occupation':
'Software Engineer'}

more_info  =  {"city":  "New  York",  "zip":
"10001"}
person.update(more_info)
print(person)   # Output: {'name': 'Alice',
'age':  30,  'country':  'USA',  'occupation':
'Software Engineer', 'city': 'New York', 'zip':
'10001'}
```

The update() method is particularly useful when you have a set of key-value pairs you want to add to an existing dictionary. It's more efficient than adding them one by one.

Removing Key-Value Pairs:

- del **Keyword:** You can remove a key-value pair using the del keyword:

Python

```python
person = {"name": "Alice", "age": 30, "city": "New York"}
del person["city"]   # Remove the "city" key-value pair
print(person)   # Output: {'name': 'Alice', 'age': 30}
```

- pop() **Method:** The pop() method removes and returns the value associated with a key:

Python

```python
person = {"name": "Alice", "age": 30, "city":
"New York"}
city = person.pop("city")   # Remove and
return the value associated with "city"
print(person)   # Output: {'name': 'Alice',
'age': 30}
print(city)  # Output: New York
```

- clear() **Method:** The clear() method
  removes all items from the dictionary:

Python

```python
person = {"name": "Alice", "age": 30, "city":
"New York"}
person.clear()
print(person)  # Output: {}
```

Accessing Keys, Values, and Items:

- keys() **Method:** The keys() method returns a view object containing the dictionary's keys:

Python

```python
person = {"name": "Alice", "age": 30, "city": "New York"}
keys = person.keys()
print(keys)   # Output: dict_keys(['name', 'age', 'city'])
for key in keys:
    print(key)  # prints each key
```

- values() **Method:** The values() method returns a view object containing the dictionary's values:

Python

```python
person = {"name": "Alice", "age": 30, "city":
"New York"}
values = personal.values()
print(values)  # Output: dict_values(['Alice',
30, 'New York'])
for value in values:
    print(value)  # prints each value
```

- items() **Method:** The items() method
  returns a view object containing the
  dictionary's key-value pairs (as
  tuples):

Python

```python
person = {"name": "Alice", "age": 30, "city":
"New York"}
items = person.items()
print(items)  # Output: dict_items([('name',
'Alice'), ('age', 30), ('city', 'New York')])
for key, value in items:
```

```python
    print(f"Key: {key}, Value: {value}")  # prints each key and value
```

These methods provide convenient ways to iterate over the keys, values, or key-value pairs in a dictionary. The view objects returned by these methods are dynamic, meaning they reflect any changes made to the dictionary.

Dictionaries are an incredibly useful data structure in Python, providing a flexible and efficient way to store and retrieve data. Understanding how to create, access, modify, and iterate over dictionaries is a fundamental skill for any Python programmer. Their ability to associate keys with values makes them ideal for representing a wide range of data, from simple mappings to complex data structures. They are a workhorse in many Python programs.

6.3 Sets: Unordered Collections of Unique Elements

Sets are another fundamental data structure in Python, characterized by two key properties: they are *unordered* and contain only *unique* elements. "Unordered" means that the elements in a set do not have a specific order; you cannot access them by index. "Unique" means that a set cannot contain duplicate values; if you try to add a duplicate, it will simply be ignored. Sets are defined by enclosing elements in curly braces {}, separated by commas. However, an empty set is created using the set() function, not {} (as this creates an empty dictionary).

Creating Sets:

Python

```
fruits = {"apple", "banana", "cherry"}  # Set of strings
numbers = {1, 2, 3, 4, 5}  # Set of integers
```

```python
mixed_set = {1, "hello", 3.14, True}  # Set of
mixed data types
empty_set = set()   # Empty set (note: {}
creates an empty dictionary)
```

Adding Elements:

You can add elements to a set using the add() method:

Python

```python
fruits = {"apple", "banana"}
fruits.add("orange")
print(fruits)   # Output: {'apple', 'banana',
'orange'} (order may vary)

fruits.add("apple") # Adding a duplicate has
no effect
print(fruits)  # Output: {'apple', 'banana',
'orange'} (no change)
```

Removing Elements:

You can remove elements from a set using the remove() method or the discard() method.

- remove(): Removes a specific element. If the element is not in the set, it raises a KeyError.

Python

```
fruits = {"apple", "banana", "orange"}
fruits.remove("banana")
print(fruits)   # Output: {'apple', 'orange'} (order may vary)

#fruits.remove("grape") # This will raise KeyError: 'grape'
```

- discard(): Removes a specific element if it is present. If the element is not in the set, it does nothing (no error).

Python

```python
fruits = {"apple", "banana", "orange"}
fruits.discard("banana")
print(fruits)   # Output: {'apple', 'orange'} (order may vary)

fruits.discard("grape")   # No error if element not found
print(fruits) # Output: {'apple', 'orange'} (no change)
```

- pop(): Removes and returns an *arbitrary* element from the set. Since sets are unordered, you can't control which element is removed. This can be useful when you need to process elements from a set one by one.

Python

```python
fruits = {"apple", "banana", "orange"}
```

```
removed_fruit = fruits.pop()
print(fruits)   # Output: {'banana', 'orange'}
or other variations
print(removed_fruit)  # Output: 'apple' or
other variations
```

- clear(): Removes all elements from the set.

Python

```
fruits = {"apple", "banana", "orange"}
fruits.clear()
print(fruits)  # Output: set()
```

6.4 Set Operations: Union, Intersection, Difference

Sets are particularly useful for performing mathematical set operations:

- **Union:** The union of two sets combines all unique elements from both sets. You can use the | operator or the union() method.

Python

```
set1 = {1, 2, 3}
set2 = {3, 4, 5}

union_set = set1 | set2   # Using the | operator
print(union_set) # Output: {1, 2, 3, 4, 5}

union_set = set1.union(set2)   # Using the union() method
print(union_set) # Output: {1, 2, 3, 4, 5}
```

- **Intersection:** The intersection of two sets returns the elements that are common to both sets. You can use the

& operator or the intersection()
method.

Python

```
set1 = {1, 2, 3}
set2 = {3, 4, 5}

intersection_set = set1 & set2  # Using the &
operator
print(intersection_set)  # Output: {3}

intersection_set = set1.intersection(set2)  #
Using the intersection() method
print(intersection_set)  # Output: {3}
```

- **Difference:** The difference of two
  sets returns the elements that are in
  the first set but not in the second set.
  You can use the - operator or the
  difference() method.

Python

```python
set1 = {1, 2, 3}
set2 = {3, 4, 5}

difference_set = set1 - set2  # Using the - operator
print(difference_set)  # Output: {1, 2}

difference_set = set1.difference(set2)  # Using the difference() method
print(difference_set)  # Output: {1, 2}

#Symmetric Difference: Elements that are in either of the sets, but not in their intersection.
symmetric_difference_set = set1 ^ set2
print(symmetric_difference_set)  # Output: {1, 2, 4, 5}
```

- **Subset and Superset:** You can check if one set is a subset or superset of another using the <= and >=

operators, or the issubset() and issuperset() methods.

Python

```python
set1 = {1, 2, 3}
set2 = {1, 2, 3, 4, 5}

print(set1 <= set2)  # Output: True (set1 is a subset of set2)
print(set2 >= set1)  # Output: True (set2 is a superset of set1)

print(set1.issubset(set2))  # Output: True
print(set2.issuperset(set1))  # Output: True
```

6.5 When to Use Which Collection Type

Choosing the right collection type depends on the specific requirements of your program:

- **Lists:** Use lists when you need an ordered, mutable sequence of items. Lists are versatile and suitable for many general-purpose tasks. Use them when order matters, and you anticipate needing to modify the collection.
- **Tuples:** Use tuples when you need an ordered, *immutable* sequence of items. Tuples are useful for representing data that should not be changed, and they can be slightly more efficient than lists. Use them when order matters, but you want to ensure the collection remains constant. Also, tuples are essential when you need to use the collection as a key in a dictionary.
- **Dictionaries:** Use dictionaries when you need to store data in key-value pairs, allowing for efficient lookups. Dictionaries are ideal for representing mappings or associations between data elements. Use them when you

need fast access to values based on a unique key.

- **Sets:** Use sets when you need an unordered collection of unique elements. Sets are useful for tasks like removing duplicates, performing set operations, and checking for membership. Use them when uniqueness is paramount, and order is not a concern. They're also highly efficient for checking if an element is present in the collection.

Understanding the strengths and weaknesses of each collection type will help you choose the most appropriate one for your specific needs. By mastering these collections, you'll be able to write more efficient, readable, and maintainable Python code. Consider the characteristics of your data and the operations you need to perform when making your choice.

CHAPTER 7

Functions: Organizing Your Code

Functions are a fundamental building block in programming, acting as self-contained blocks of code designed to perform specific tasks. They are essential for organizing your code, making it more modular, reusable, and easier to understand. This chapter delves into the intricacies of defining functions, working with arguments and parameters, and utilizing return values effectively.

7.1 Defining Functions

Defining a function in Python involves using the def keyword, followed by the function name, parentheses (), and a colon :. The code block that makes up the function's body is indented.

Python

```
def function_name(parameters):
    """Docstring: Description of the function's
purpose."""
    # Code to execute
    # ...
```

- def: Keyword used to define a function.
- function_name: The name you give to your function. Choose descriptive names that indicate the function's purpose. Follow the same naming conventions as for variables (lowercase with underscores for separation).
- parameters (optional): Input values that the function can receive. They are listed inside the parentheses, separated by commas.
- Docstring: An optional but highly recommended string that describes the function's purpose, arguments,

and return values. It's enclosed in triple quotes """.

- Code block: The indented block of code that performs the function's task.

Example:

Python

```python
def greet(name):
    """Greets the person passed in as a parameter."""
    print(f"Hello, {name}!")

greet("Alice")  # Output: Hello, Alice!
greet("Bob")    # Output: Hello, Bob!
```

This defines a function called greet that takes one parameter, name. When the function is called, the value of name is used in the print statement.

7.2 Function Arguments and Parameters

- **Parameters:** Parameters are the variables defined inside the parentheses of the function definition. They act as placeholders for the values the function expects to receive.
- **Arguments:** Arguments are the actual values that you pass to the function when you call it. They correspond to the parameters in the function definition.

Python

```python
def add(x, y):  # x and y are parameters
    """Adds two numbers and prints the sum."""
    sum = x + y
    print(sum)

add(5, 3)  # 5 and 3 are arguments
```

```python
add(10, 7) # 10 and 7 are arguments
```

Types of Arguments:

Python supports different types of arguments:

- **Positional Arguments:** Arguments are passed in the order they are defined in the function definition.
- **Keyword Arguments:** Arguments are passed with the parameter name specified. This allows you to pass arguments in any order.

Python

```python
def describe_person(name, age, city):
    print(f"Name: {name}, Age: {age}, City: {city}")
```

```
describe_person("Alice", 30, "New York")  #
Positional arguments
describe_person(age=30, city="New York",
name="Alice")  # Keyword arguments
```

- **Default Arguments:** You can provide default values for parameters in the function definition. If an argument is not passed for that parameter when the function is called, the default value is used.

Python

```
def power(base, exponent=2):  # exponent
has a default value of 2
    result = base ** exponent
    print(result)

power(5)    # Output: 25 (exponent uses the
default value)
```

```python
power(5, 3)    # Output: 125 (exponent is
explicitly set to 3)
```

- **Variable-Length Arguments:** You can define functions that accept a variable number of arguments using *args (for positional arguments) and **kwargs (for keyword arguments).[1]

Python

```python
def print_numbers(*args):
  for num in args:
    print(num)

print_numbers(1, 2, 3, 4, 5)  # Output: 1 2 3
4 5

def print_info(**kwargs):
  for key, value in kwargs.items():
    print(f"{key}: {value}")
```

```python
print_info(name="Bob",            age=25,
city="London")  # Output: name: Bob, age:
25, city: London
```

7.3 Return Values

Functions can return a value using the return statement. When a return statement is encountered, the function execution stops, and the specified value is returned to the caller.

Python

```python
def add(x, y):
    """Adds two numbers and returns the sum."""
    sum = x + y
    return sum


result = add(5, 3)
print(result)  # Output: 8
```

A function can return any data type, including multiple values (as a tuple):

Python

```python
def calculate_area_and_perimeter(length, width):
    area = length * width
    perimeter = 2 * (length + width)
    return area, perimeter  # Returns a tuple of two values

area, perimeter = calculate_area_and_perimeter(10, 5)
print(f"Area: {area}, Perimeter: {perimeter}")  # Output: Area: 50, Perimeter: 30
```

If a function does not have a return statement, it implicitly returns None.

Python

```python
def do_something():
    print("Doing something...")

result = do_something()
print(result)  # Output: None
```

Functions are essential for writing modular, reusable, and maintainable code. They allow you to break down complex problems into smaller, more manageable pieces. By mastering functions, you'll be able to write more organized and efficient Python programs. Understanding how to define functions, work with arguments and parameters, and utilize return values is a crucial step in your programming journey. Remember to write clear and concise docstrings to document your functions, making them easier to understand and use.

7.4 Scope and Lifetime of Variables

The scope of a variable refers to the region of your code where that variable can be accessed.[1] The lifetime of a variable refers to how long it exists in memory during the execution of your program.[2] Understanding scope and lifetime is crucial for preventing naming conflicts and ensuring that your variables behave as expected.[3]

Scope:

Python has several scoping rules, but the most important ones to understand are:

- **Local Scope:** Variables defined inside a function have local scope.[4] They are only accessible within that function.[5] When the function finishes executing, the local variables are destroyed.[6]

Python

```python
def my_function():
    x = 10  # x has local scope
    print(x)

my_function()  # Output: 10
# print(x)   # This will raise a NameError:
name 'x' is not defined (x is not accessible
outside the function)
```

- **Global Scope:** Variables defined outside any function have global scope.[7] They can be accessed from anywhere in your code, including inside functions.[8]

Python

```python
y = 20  # y has global scope

def another_function():
    print(y)
```

```
another_function()  # Output: 20
print(y)  # Output: 20
```

- **Nonlocal Scope (for nested functions):** If you have a function nested inside another function, the inner function can access variables from the outer function's scope, but it needs to be explicitly declared as nonlocal.

Python

```
def outer_function():
    z = 30  # z is in the outer function's scope
    def inner_function():
        nonlocal z  # Declare that we're using z from the outer scope
        z = 40  # Modifying z in the inner function affects z in the outer function
        print(z)
```

```
inner_function() # Output: 40
print(z) # Output: 40 (z was changed by
the inner function)

outer_function()
```

- **LEGB Rule (Local, Enclosing, Global, Built-in):** Python's scope resolution follows the LEGB rule.[9] When a variable is referenced, Python searches for it in this order: Local, Enclosing (nonlocal), Global, and Built-in (e.g., print, len).

Lifetime:

The lifetime of a variable is tied to its scope.[10]

- Local variables exist only while the function is executing.[11] They are created when the function is called and destroyed when the function returns.[12]

- Global variables exist for the duration of the program's execution.[13] They are created when the program starts and destroyed when the program ends.[14]

7.5 Docstrings and Function Annotations

- **Docstrings:** Docstrings (documentation strings) are multiline strings used to document your functions.[15] They are enclosed in triple quotes """ and should describe the function's purpose, arguments, and return values. Good docstrings are essential for making your code understandable and maintainable.[16]

Python

```python
def add(x, y):
```

```
"""
Adds two numbers.

Args:
    x: The first number.
    y: The second number.

Returns:
    The sum of x and y.
"""

return x + y


help(add)  # Prints the docstring
```

- **Function Annotations:** Function annotations are a way to add metadata to function parameters and return values.[17] They don't affect the function's execution but can be used by external tools for type checking or other purposes. Annotations are written using a colon : after the parameter name and -> before the return value.

```python
def greet(name: str) -> str:
    """Greets a person."""
    return f"Hello, {name}!"

print(greet("Alice"))  # Output: Hello, Alice!
print(greet.__annotations__)  # Output:
{'name': <class 'str'>, 'return': <class 'str'>}
```

Annotations are particularly helpful for static analysis tools that can help catch type errors in your code.[18] They also serve as a form of documentation, clearly indicating the expected types of data a function works with.

7.6 Modularizing Your Code with Functions

Modularizing your code with functions is a crucial aspect of writing clean, maintainable, and reusable code.[19] By breaking down your program into smaller, self-contained functions, you achieve several benefits:

- **Improved Readability:** Functions make your code easier to read and understand. Each function performs a specific task, making the overall logic of your program clearer.
- **Code Reusability:** Functions can be reused in different parts of your program or even in other programs. This reduces code duplication and saves development time.[20]
- **Easier Debugging:** When your code is modularized, it's easier to isolate and debug problems.[21] You can test

each function independently to ensure it's working correctly.

- **Better Organization:** Functions help you organize your code logically. Related functions can be grouped together, making your codebase more structured.[22]
- **Collaboration:** Modular code is easier to work on collaboratively.[23] Different developers can work on different functions without interfering with each other's code.

Example: A program to calculate the area and perimeter of multiple rectangles:

Python

```python
def calculate_area(length, width):
    return length * width

def calculate_perimeter(length, width):
    return 2 * (length + width)
```

```python
def print_rectangle_info(length, width):
    area = calculate_area(length, width)
    perimeter = calculate_perimeter(length, width)
    print(f"Length: {length}, Width: {width}, Area: {area}, Perimeter: {perimeter}")

rectangles = [(5, 10), (3, 7), (8, 12)]

for length, width in rectangles:
    print_rectangle_info(length, width)
```

In this example, the code is broken down into three functions: calculate_area, calculate_perimeter, and print_rectangle_info. This makes the code more organized, readable, and reusable. If you need to calculate the area or perimeter of other rectangles, you can simply call the corresponding functions. This example illustrates the power of functions in modularizing and organizing your code. They are not just about avoiding repetition, but also about creating logical blocks of functionality that make your programs easier to reason about, maintain, and extend.

CHAPTER 8

Input and Output

This chapter explores how Python interacts with the outside world, specifically focusing on input and output operations. Mastering these techniques is essential for creating programs that can receive data from users, display results, and work with files.[1] We'll cover reading input from the user, printing formatted output to the console, and the crucial skill of reading and writing data to files.

8.1 Reading Input from the User

Python provides the input() function to read input from the user. The input() function displays a prompt to the user and waits for them to enter text. The entered text is then returned as a string.[2]

Python

```
name = input("Enter your name: ")
print(f"Hello, {name}!")

age_str = input("Enter your age: ")
age = int(age_str)   # Convert the input
string to an integer
print(f"You are {age} years old.")
```

Important Considerations:

- **Input is always a string:** Even if the user enters a number, the input() function returns it as a string. You'll often need to convert the input to the appropriate data type (e.g., using int(), float(), or bool()).
- **Prompts:** The prompt you provide to the input() function should be clear and informative, telling the user what kind of input is expected.

- **Error Handling:** It's a good practice to include error handling (e.g., using try-except blocks) to handle cases where the user might enter invalid input (e.g., trying to convert a non-numeric string to an integer).

Python

```python
while True:
  try:
    age_str = input("Enter your age: ")
    age = int(age_str)
    if age > 0:
      break
    else:
        print("Age must be a positive integer.")
  except ValueError:
      print("Invalid input. Please enter a number.")

print(f"Your age is {age}.")
```

8.2 Printing Output to the Console

Python provides the print() function to display output to the console. You can print strings, numbers, and other data types.[3]

Python

```python
print("Hello, World!")
print(10 + 5)  # Output: 15
print("The answer is", 42)  # Output: The answer is 42
```

Formatting Output:

Python offers several ways to format output:[4]

- **f-strings (Formatted String Literals):** f-strings are the most modern and convenient way to format strings.[5] You can embed expressions inside curly braces {} within the string.

Python

```
name = "Alice"
age = 30
print(f"My name is {name} and I am {age} years old.")  # Output: My name is Alice and I am 30 years old.
```

- str.format() **Method:** The format() method provides more control over formatting.

Python

```
name = "Bob"
```

```python
score = 100
print("Name: {}, Score: {}".format(name,
score))  # Output: Name: Bob, Score: 100
print("Name: {0}, Score: {1}".format(name,
score))  # Output: Name: Bob, Score: 100
(explicit indexing)
print("Name: {name}, Score:
{score}".format(name=name, score=score))
# Output: Name: Bob, Score: 100 (keyword
arguments)
```

- % **Operator (Old Style Formatting):** This is an older style of formatting that is still supported but less preferred.[6]

Python

```python
name = "Charlie"
percentage = 95.5
```

```python
print("Name: %s, Percentage: %.2f" % (name, percentage))   # Output: Name: Charlie, Percentage: 95.50
```

Controlling Output:

- end **Parameter:** The print() function automatically adds a newline character at the end of the output. You can change this behavior using the end parameter.

Python

```python
print("Hello", end=" ")   # Prints "Hello" followed by a space instead of a newline
print("World!") # Output: Hello World!
```

- sep **Parameter:** The sep parameter allows you to specify the separator between multiple items printed in a single print() call.

Python

```
print("Apple", "Banana", "Cherry", sep=", ")
# Output: Apple, Banana, Cherry
```

8.3 Working with Files: Reading and Writing

Working with files is essential for storing and retrieving data persistently.[7] Python provides built-in functions for reading and writing files.[8]

Opening Files:

You must open a file before you can read from it or write to it. The open() function takes two arguments: the file path and the mode.

Python

```python
file = open("my_file.txt", "r")   # Open for reading ("r" mode)
file = open("my_file.txt", "w")   # Open for writing ("w" mode) - overwrites the file if it exists, creates if it doesn't
file = open("my_file.txt", "a")   # Open for appending ("a" mode) - adds to the end of the file
file = open("my_file.txt", "x")   # Open for exclusive creation ("x" mode) - fails if the file exists
file = open("my_file.txt", "r+")  # Open for both reading and writing
file = open("my_file.txt", "w+")  # Open for both reading and writing (overwrites or creates the file)
file = open("my_file.txt", "a+")  # Open for both reading and appending
```

Reading Files:

- read(): Reads the entire contents of the file as a single string.

Python

```python
with open("my_file.txt", "r") as file:
    content = file.read()
    print(content)
```

- readline(): **Reads one line at a time.**

Python

```python
with open("my_file.txt", "r") as file:
    line = file.readline()
    while line:
        print(line, end="") # end="" to prevent double newlines
        line = file.readline()
```

- readlines(): **Reads all lines into a list of strings.**

Python

```python
with open("my_file.txt", "r") as file:
    lines = file.readlines()
    for line in lines:
        print(line, end="") # end="" to prevent
double newlines
```

Writing Files:

- write(): Writes a string to the file.

Python

```python
with open("my_file.txt", "w") as file:
    file.write("Hello, World!\n")
    file.write("This is a new line.\n")
```

- writelines(): Writes a list of strings to the file.

Python

```
lines = ["Line 1\n", "Line 2\n", "Line 3\n"]
with open("my_file.txt", "w") as file:
    file.writelines(lines)
```

Closing Files:

It's crucial to close files after you're finished with them to release system resources. The with statement ensures that files are closed automatically, even if errors occur. It's the recommended way to work with files.

Python

```
with open("my_file.txt", "r") as file: # File is
automatically closed after the block is
exited.
    content = file.read()


# file.closed will return True after the with
block.
```

Working with input and output, including files, is a fundamental part of programming.[9] These skills allow you to create interactive programs that can process data, store it, and communicate with the user. Mastering file I/O is crucial for building applications that handle persistent data and interact with the file system. Remember to always handle potential errors, especially with file operations, to ensure your programs are robust and reliable.

8.3.2 Reading Data from Files 8.

8.3.1 Opening and Closing Files

Before you can work with a file (read from it or write to it), you must first *open* it. Python's open() function is used for this purpose. It takes the file path as its primary argument and a *mode* argument that specifies how the file should be opened.

File Modes:

Mode	Description
'r"	Read mode (default). Opens the file for reading. Raises an error if the file does not exist.
'w"	Write mode. Opens the file for writing. If the file exists, it overwrites the contents. If the file does not exist, it creates a new file.
'a"	Append mode. Opens the file for writing, but it adds to the end of the file. If the file does not exist, it creates a new file.

"x"	Exclusive creation mode. Creates a new file, but fails if the file already exists.
"b"	Binary mode. Used to handle non-text files (e.g., images, audio) Combine with other modes (e.g., "rb", "wb").
"t"	Text mode (default). Used to handle text files.
"+"	Update mode. Opens the file for both reading and writing. Combine with other modes (e.g., "r+", "w+", "a+").

Opening a File:

Python

```python
file = open("my_file.txt", "r")    # Open
"my_file.txt" in read mode
```

Closing a File:

It's essential to close the file after you're finished with it to release system resources. You can close a file using the close() method:

Python

```python
file.close()
```

The with Statement (Recommended):

The best practice for working with files is to use the with statement. This ensures that the file is automatically closed, even if errors occur.

Python

```python
with open("my_file.txt", "r") as file:
```

```
  # Code to work with the file
        contents = file.read() # File is
automatically closed when the 'with' block is
exited.

# file.closed will return True after the with
block.
```

The with statement creates a context, and
when the context is exited (either normally
or due to an exception), the file is
automatically closed. This prevents resource
leaks and potential data corruption.

8.3.2 Reading Data from Files

Once a file is open in read mode (or a mode
that allows reading), you can read its
contents using various methods:

- read(): Reads the entire file content as
  a single string.

Python

```python
with open("my_file.txt", "r") as file:
    content = file.read()
    print(content)
```

- readline(): Reads one line at a time.

Python

```python
with open("my_file.txt", "r") as file:
    line = file.readline()
    while line:
        print(line, end="")  # end="" prevents double newlines
        line = file.readline()
```

- readlines(): Reads all lines into a list of strings.

Python

```
with open("my_file.txt", "r") as file:
    lines = file.readlines()
    for line in lines:
        print(line, end="")  # end="" prevents
double newlines
```

8.3.3 Writing Data to Files

To write data to a file, you must open it in write mode ("w"), append mode ("a"), or update mode ("r+", "w+", "a+").

- write(): Writes a string to the file.

Python

```
with open("my_file.txt", "w") as file:
    file.write("Hello, World!\n")
    file.write("This is a new line.\n")
```

- writelines(): Writes a list of strings to the file.

Python

```
lines = ["Line 1\n", "Line 2\n", "Line 3\n"]
with open("my_file.txt", "w") as file:
    file.writelines(lines)
```

Important Notes for Writing:

- "w" **mode:** Overwrites the file if it exists. Be cautious when using this mode.
- "a" **mode:** Appends to the end of the file.
- **Newlines:** You need to explicitly add newline characters (\n) to create new lines in the file.

8.4 Formatting Output

Formatting output is essential to present information clearly and effectively. Python provides several formatting techniques:

- **f-strings (Formatted String Literals):** f-strings are the most modern and convenient way to format strings. You can embed expressions inside curly braces {} within the string.

Python

```
name = "Alice"
age = 30
print(f"My name is {name} and I am {age} years old.")
```

- str.format() **Method:** The format() method gives you more control over formatting.

Python

```
name = "Bob"
score = 100
print("Name: {}, Score: {}".format(name, score))  # Using placeholders
print("Name: {0}, Score: {1}".format(name, score))  # Using indices
print("Name: {name}, Score: {score}".format(name=name, score=score))  # Using keyword arguments
```

- **% Operator (Old Style Formatting):** This is an older style that is still supported but less preferred.

Python

```
name = "Charlie"
percentage = 95.5
```

```python
print("Name: %s, Percentage: %.2f" %
(name, percentage))  # %s for string, %.2f
for float with 2 decimal places
```

- **Controlling Output:**
  - end **Parameter:** The print()
    function automatically adds a
    newline character at the end.
    Use end="" to suppress this.
- Python

```python
print("Hello", end=" ")
print("World!")  # Output: Hello World!
```

-
  - sep **Parameter:** Specify the
    separator between multiple
    items printed in a single print()
    call.
- Python

```
print("Apple", "Banana", "Cherry", sep=", ")
# Output: Apple, Banana, Cherry
```

-
-

Formatting output is a crucial part of making your programs user-friendly and presenting information in a clear and structured way. Understanding the different formatting options allows you to choose the most appropriate method for your needs. The with statement and proper file handling are vital for robust and reliable file processing. By combining these techniques, you can create Python programs that effectively interact with the user, process data, and manage files.

CHAPTER 9

Error Handling and Debugging

Writing error-free code is a challenging but essential aspect of programming. Errors are inevitable, but knowing how to handle them gracefully and debug your code effectively is what separates a novice programmer from a proficient one. This chapter delves into the different types of errors you'll encounter in Python, introduces exception handling mechanisms, and explores debugging techniques to help you write robust and reliable code.

9.1 Types of Errors: Syntax Errors, Runtime Errors, Logical Errors

Errors in programming can be broadly classified into three categories:

- **Syntax Errors:** These errors occur when you violate the grammatical rules of the Python language.[1] The interpreter detects syntax errors before the program execution begins.[2] They are typically the easiest to fix because the interpreter provides a clear message indicating the location and nature of the error.

Python

```
# Syntax Error Example
print "Hello, world!" # Missing parentheses
```

Python will immediately flag this error, pointing to the missing parentheses.

- **Runtime Errors:** These errors occur during the execution of the program.[3] The interpreter can't detect them before the program runs. Runtime errors often arise from unexpected input or conditions that the program wasn't designed to handle.

Python

```
# Runtime Error Example
result = 10 / 0  # Division by zero
```

This code will compile without issues, but when it runs, a ZeroDivisionError will be raised.

- **Logical Errors:** These are the most subtle and challenging type of error.[4] Logical errors occur when your code runs without crashing but produces incorrect results.[5] They arise from flaws in the program's logic or algorithm.

Python

```python
# Logical Error Example
def calculate_average(numbers):
    total = sum(numbers)
    average = total / len(numbers) + 1 # Incorrect logic
    return average
```

This code will run without errors, but the calculated average will be incorrect due to the added + 1. Logical errors require careful testing and debugging to identify.

9.2 Exception Handling: try, except, finally

Python provides a powerful mechanism called exception handling to deal with runtime errors gracefully.[6] Instead of crashing the program, you can anticipate potential errors and write code to handle them. The key keywords used in exception handling are try, except, and finally.

- try **Block:** The try block contains the code that you suspect might raise an exception.
- except **Block:** The except block contains the code that will be executed if a specific exception occurs in the corresponding try block. You can have multiple except blocks to handle different types of exceptions.
- finally **Block (Optional):** The finally block contains code that will be executed *regardless* of whether an exception occurs in the try block. This is often used for cleanup tasks, such as closing files or releasing resources.[7]

Example:

Python

```
try:
    number = int(input("Enter a number: "))
    result = 10 / number
    print(f"The result is: {result}")
```

```
except ZeroDivisionError:
    print("Error: Division by zero is not
allowed.")
except ValueError:
    print("Error: Invalid input. Please enter a
number.")
finally:
    print("This block always executes.")

print("Program continues...") # This will
execute even if there is an exception.
```

Explanation:

1. The code inside the try block is executed.
2. If a ZeroDivisionError occurs (e.g., the user enters 0), the first except block is executed.
3. If a ValueError occurs (e.g., the user enters text instead of a number), the second except block is executed.

4. If any other exception occurs, and there is no matching except block, the program will terminate.
5. The code in the finally block is *always* executed, regardless of whether an exception occurred.
6. The code after the try-except-finally block continues to execute.

Handling Multiple Exceptions:

You can handle multiple exceptions with separate except blocks or by grouping them:

Python

```
try:
    # ... code that might raise exceptions ...
except (ZeroDivisionError, ValueError):   # Grouping exceptions
    print("Error: Invalid input or division by zero.")
except FileNotFoundError:
    print("Error: File not found.")
```

else **Clause:**

You can also include an else clause with a try-except block. The code in the else block will be executed only if *no* exceptions occur in the try block.

Python

```
try:
    file = open("my_file.txt", "r")
except FileNotFoundError:
    print("File not found.")
else:   # This will execute only if the file is found.
    content = file.read()
    print(content)
    file.close() # Close the file inside the else block.
```

Raising Exceptions:

You can also explicitly raise exceptions in your code using the raise keyword. This can be useful for signaling errors or exceptional conditions that your code detects.

Python

```python
def divide(x, y):
    if y == 0:
        raise ZeroDivisionError("Cannot divide by zero.")
    return x / y


try:
    result = divide(10, 0)
except ZeroDivisionError as e:
    print(f"An error occurred: {e}")
```

Exception handling is a crucial skill in Python.[8] It allows you to write more robust and fault-tolerant code by anticipating potential errors and providing appropriate responses.[9] By using try, except, and finally blocks effectively, you can prevent your programs from crashing and provide a more user-friendly experience. Understanding how to raise exceptions allows you to signal errors in your functions and enforce certain conditions. Mastering these techniques will significantly improve the quality and reliability of your Python programs.

9.3 Raising Exceptions

While Python provides built-in exceptions for common errors, you can also create and raise your own custom exceptions.[1] This is particularly useful when you want to signal specific error conditions within your code or create more descriptive error messages.[2]

Creating Custom Exceptions:

You can create a custom exception by defining a new class that inherits from the built-in Exception class or one of its subclasses.[3]

Python

```python
class InvalidInputError(Exception):
    """Custom exception raised for invalid input."""
    def __init__(self, message, value):
        self.message = message
        self.value = value
        super().__init__(self.message)   # Initialize the base Exception class

    def __str__(self): # Override the __str__
method to customize error message.
        return f"{self.message}: {self.value}"


def process_data(data):
    if not isinstance(data, list):
        raise InvalidInputError("Data must be a list.", data)
    # ... process the data ...

try:
    process_data("not a list")
except InvalidInputError as e:
```

```python
    print(f"Error: {e}") # Output: Error: Data
must be a list.: not a list

try:
  process_data([1,2,3])
except InvalidInputError as e:
  print(f"Error: {e}") # No error.
```

Raising Exceptions:

You raise an exception using the raise keyword, followed by the exception object.

Python

```python
def check_value(value):
    if value < 0:
            raise ValueError("Value must be
non-negative.")
    # ... proceed with the function ...

try:
    check_value(-5)
```

```python
except ValueError as e:
    print(f"Error: {e}")  # Output: Error:
Value must be non-negative.
```

Chaining Exceptions (Python 3):

In Python 3 and later, you can chain exceptions using the from keyword. This allows you to provide more context about the original exception that caused the current exception.

Python

```python
try:
    # ... some code that might raise an
IOError ...
    with open("nonexistent_file.txt", "r") as f:
        pass
except FileNotFoundError as e1:
    try:
        # ... handle the IOError and potentially
raise a new exception ...
```

```
    raise IOError("Failed to open file.")
from e1 # Chaining the exception
  except IOError as e2:
    print(f"An error occurred: {e2}")
    print(f"Original exception: {e1}")
```

9.4 Debugging Techniques: Using Print Statements, Debuggers

Debugging is the process of identifying and fixing errors in your code.[4] Here are some common debugging techniques:

- **Print Statements:** The simplest debugging technique is to use print() statements to track the values of variables and the flow of your program. Print statements can help you pinpoint where the error is occurring.[5]

Python

```python
def my_function(x):
    print(f"Entering my_function with x = {x}")
    y = x * 2
    print(f"y = {y}")
    return y

result = my_function(5)
print(f"Result = {result}")
```

- **Debuggers:** Debuggers are powerful tools that allow you to step through your code line by line, inspect variables, set breakpoints, and evaluate expressions. Python has a built-in debugger (pdb), and most IDEs (like VS Code, PyCharm) have integrated debuggers.

Using the pdb Debugger:

Python

```python
import pdb

def my_function(x):
    pdb.set_trace()  # Set a breakpoint
    y = x * 2
    return y

result = my_function(5)
print(result)
```

When you run this code, the program will stop at the pdb.set_trace() line. You can then use pdb commands (like n for next line, s for step into, c for continue, p to print a variable's value, q to quit) to control the execution and inspect the program's state.

Using IDE Debuggers:

IDE debuggers are generally easier to use than pdb. You can set breakpoints by clicking in the margin next to the line of code, and then use the debugger controls to step through the code, inspect variables, and evaluate expressions. Consult your IDE's documentation for specific instructions.

9.5 Common Python Errors and How to Fix Them

Here are some common Python errors and how to fix them:

- NameError: This error occurs when you try to use a variable that has not been defined.[6] Make sure you have assigned a value to the variable before using it.
- TypeError: This error occurs when you try to perform an operation on incompatible data types (e.g., adding a string to an integer).[7] Use type conversion functions (like int(), float(), str()) to convert the data types if necessary.

- ValueError: This error occurs when you try to convert a value to a specific data type, but the value is not compatible (e.g., trying to convert "hello" to an integer).[8]
- IndexError: This error occurs when you try to access an element in a sequence (like a list or string) using an index that is out of range.[9] Make sure your index is within the valid range (0 to length - 1).
- KeyError: This error occurs when you try to access a key in a dictionary that does not exist.[10] Use the get() method to avoid this error or check if the key exists before accessing it.
- AttributeError: This error occurs when you try to access an attribute (method or variable) of an object that does not have that attribute.[11] Make sure the object you are working with has the attribute you are trying to access.

- FileNotFoundError: This error occurs when you try to open a file that does not exist.[12] Double-check the file path and make sure the file is in the correct location.
- ZeroDivisionError: This error occurs when you try to divide a number by zero.[13] Check your code for potential division by zero errors and handle them appropriately.

CHAPTER 10

Object-Oriented Programming (OOP) Fundamentals

Object-Oriented Programming (OOP) is a programming paradigm that organizes software design around "objects," which are instances of[1] "classes."[2] OOP offers a powerful and intuitive way to structure code, making it more modular, reusable, and easier to maintain.[3] This chapter introduces the fundamental concepts of OOP, focusing on classes and objects, and how to define them in Python.

10.1 Introduction to OOP Concepts: Classes and Objects

OOP revolves around the concepts of classes and objects:[4]

- **Class:** A class is a blueprint or template for creating objects. It defines the properties (attributes) and behaviors (methods) that objects of that class will have.[6] Think of a class[7] as a cookie cutter – it defines the shape and features of the cookies you create.

- **Object (Instance):** An object is a specific instance of a class. It's a concrete realization of the class's blueprint. Objects have their own unique data (values for the attributes) and can perform the actions defined by the class's methods.[8] Think of an object as a specific cookie created using the cookie cutter. Each cookie has its own characteristics (e.g., color, size), even though they all share the same shape.

Key Principles of OOP:

OOP is based on several key principles:[9]

- **Encapsulation:** Encapsulation bundles data (attributes) and the code that operates on that data (methods) within an object.[10] It hides the internal implementation details of the object and exposes only a well-defined interface for interacting with it.[11] This protects the data from accidental modification and makes the code more modular.[12]
- **Inheritance:** Inheritance allows you to create new classes (derived classes or subclasses) based on existing classes (base classes or superclasses). The derived class inherits the attributes and methods of the base

class[13] and can add its own unique properties or override existing ones.[14] This promotes code reuse and allows you to create hierarchies of classes.[15]

- **Polymorphism:** Polymorphism (meaning "many forms") allows objects of different classes to be treated as objects of a common type.[16] This enables you to write code that can work with objects of various classes without needing to know their specific type. Polymorphism makes your code more flexible and extensible.[17]

- **Abstraction:** Abstraction focuses on the essential characteristics of an object and ignores the irrelevant details.[18] It simplifies complex systems by providing a high-level view of the objects and their interactions.[19] Abstraction helps you manage complexity and makes your code easier to understand.[20]

10.2 Defining Classes

In Python, you define a class using the class keyword, followed by the class name (using CamelCase convention) and a colon :. The class body contains the definitions of the attributes and methods.

Python

```python
class Dog:  # Class name (CamelCase)
    """A class representing a dog."""

    def __init__(self, name, breed):  # Constructor (initializer)
        self.name = name  # Instance attribute (data)
        self.breed = breed  # Instance attribute (data)

    def bark(self):  # Method (behavior)
        print("Woof!")
```

```
def describe(self):
    print(f"Name: {self.name}, Breed:
{self.breed}")
```

Explanation:

- class Dog:: Defines a class named Dog.
- __init__(self, name, breed): This is the constructor (or initializer) of the class. It's a special method that is automatically called when you create a new object of the class. The self parameter refers to the instance of the class being created. name and breed are parameters that are used to initialize the object's attributes.
- self.name = name: Creates an instance attribute named name and assigns it the value passed as an argument. Instance attributes store the data associated with each object.[21]

- self.breed = breed: Creates an instance attribute named breed and assigns it the value passed as an argument.
- bark(self) and describe(self): These are methods (functions) defined within the class. They represent the behaviors or actions that objects of the Dog class can perform. The self parameter is automatically passed to the method when it is called on an object.

Creating Objects (Instances):

You create an object (instance) of a class by calling the class name as if it were a function, passing the required arguments to the constructor.[22]

Python

```
my_dog    =    Dog("Buddy",    "Golden
Retriever") # Create a Dog object
```

```python
another_dog = Dog("Max", "German Shepherd") # Create another Dog object
```

Accessing Attributes and Calling Methods:

You can access an object's attributes using the dot notation:

Python

```python
print(my_dog.name) # Output: Buddy
print(another_dog.breed)    # Output: German Shepherd
```

You can call an object's methods using the dot notation as well:

Python

```python
my_dog.bark() # Output: Woof!
another_dog.describe()   # Output: Name: Max, Breed: German Shepherd
```

self:

The self parameter is a crucial part of defining classes and methods in Python. It's a reference to the instance of the class on which the method is being called. When you call a method on an object (e.g., my_dog.bark()), Python automatically passes the object itself as the first argument to the method. By convention, this first argument is named self. Inside the method, you use self to access the object's attributes and other methods.

This introduction to classes and objects lays the foundation for understanding the power and elegance of object-oriented programming. By mastering these fundamental concepts, you can begin to design and implement more complex and maintainable software systems. In the following sections, we'll delve deeper into the other core principles of OOP: inheritance, polymorphism, and abstraction.

10.3 Creating Objects (Instances)

Creating an object, also known as instantiation, is the process of bringing a class to life.[1] It's like using the cookie cutter (the class) to make an actual cookie (the object). In Python, you create an object by calling the class name as if it were a function.[2] This call invokes the class's constructor (__init__ method), which initializes the object's attributes.

Python

```
my_dog = Dog("Buddy", "Golden Retriever")
your_dog = Dog("Max", "German Shepherd")
```

In this example:

- my_dog and your_dog are objects (instances) of the Dog class.
- "Buddy" and "Golden Retriever" are arguments passed to the Dog class constructor to initialize the name and breed attributes of my_dog.
- "Max" and "German Shepherd" are arguments passed to the Dog class constructor to initialize the name and breed attributes of your_dog.

Each object created from a class is independent and has its own set of attribute values.[3] So, my_dog has the name "Buddy" and breed "Golden Retriever," while your_dog has the name "Max" and breed "German Shepherd."

10.4 Attributes and Methods

Classes define two fundamental components: attributes and methods.[4]

- **Attributes:** Attributes are the data associated with an object. They represent the object's properties or characteristics.[5] In the Dog class example, name and breed are attributes. Each Dog object has its own unique values for these attributes.
- **Methods:** Methods are functions defined within a class.[6] They represent the actions or behaviors that objects of the class can perform. In the[7] Dog class, bark() and describe() are methods.

Accessing Attributes:

You can access an object's attributes using the dot notation:

Python

```
print(my_dog.name)  # Output: Buddy
print(your_dog.breed)  # Output: German Shepherd
```

Calling Methods:

You can call an object's methods using the dot notation as well:

Python

```
my_dog.bark()  # Output: Woof!
your_dog.describe()  # Output: Name: Max, Breed: German Shepherd
```

10.5 The self Keyword

The self keyword is a crucial part of defining classes and methods in Python. It's a reference to the instance of the class on which the method is being called. When you call a method on an object (e.g., my_dog.bark()), Python automatically passes the object itself as the first argument to the method. By convention, this first argument is named self.

Inside the method, you use self to access the object's attributes and other methods. For example, in the Dog class:

Python

```python
def describe(self):
        print(f"Name: {self.name}, Breed: {self.breed}")
```

self.name refers to the name attribute of the specific Dog object on which the describe() method is called. Without self, the method wouldn't know which object's name attribute to access.

10.6 Introduction to Inheritance and Polymorphism

Inheritance and polymorphism are two of the most powerful features of object-oriented programming.[8]

Inheritance:

Inheritance allows you to create new classes (derived classes or subclasses) based on existing classes (base classes or superclasses). The derived class inherits the attributes and methods of the base class and can add its own unique properties or override existing ones.[10] This promotes code reuse and allows you to create hierarchies of classes.

Example:

Python

```
class Puppy(Dog):   # Puppy inherits from
Dog
        def __init__(self, name, breed,
is_trained):
        super().__init__(name, breed) # Call
the parent class's constructor
        self.is_trained = is_trained

    def learn_trick(self, trick):
        print(f"{self.name} learned the {trick}
trick!")
```

Puppy inherits from Dog. It has all the attributes and methods of Dog (like name, breed, bark(), describe()) and adds its own attributes (like is_trained) and methods (like learn_trick()).

Polymorphism:

Polymorphism (meaning "many forms") allows objects of different classes to be treated as objects of a common type. This enables you to write code that can work with objects of various classes without needing to know their specific type. Polymorphism makes your code more flexible and extensible.[11]

Example:

Python

```python
def dog_greeting(dog):   # Can accept both Dog and Puppy objects
  dog.bark()

my_dog   =   Dog("Buddy",   "Golden Retriever")
my_puppy = Puppy("Sparky", "Labrador", True)

dog_greeting(my_dog) # Output: Woof!
dog_greeting(my_puppy) # Output: Woof!
```

Even though my_dog is a Dog and my_puppy is a Puppy, the dog_greeting() function can accept both because Puppy *is a*

Dog (due to inheritance). This is an example of polymorphism.

Inheritance and polymorphism are powerful tools for creating complex and maintainable software systems.[12] They allow you to model real-world relationships between objects and write code that is adaptable to change.[13] Understanding these concepts is essential for mastering object-oriented programming.

CHAPTER 11

Working with Modules and Package

As your Python programs grow in complexity, organizing your code into manageable units becomes crucial. Modules and packages provide a powerful mechanism for structuring your code, promoting reusability, and improving maintainability.[1] This chapter delves into how to work with modules and packages, covering importing modules, utilizing built-in modules, and creating your own custom modules and packages.

11.1 Importing Modules

A module is a file containing Python code (functions, classes, variables, etc.). Modules allow you to organize related code into separate files, making your codebase more structured and easier to navigate.[2] To use the code in a module, you need to *import* it into your current script.[3]

Import Statements:

Python provides several ways to import modules:[4]

- import module_name: This imports the entire module.[5] You then access the module's contents using the dot notation (module_name.item).

Python

```python
import math

result = math.sqrt(25)  # Access the sqrt() function from the math module
print(result) # Output: 5.0
```

- import module_name as alias: This imports the module and assigns it an alias (a different name). This can be useful for shortening long module names or avoiding naming conflicts.[6]

Python

```
import math as m

result = m.sqrt(25)
print(result)  # Output: 5.0
```

- from module_name import item: This imports a specific item (function, class, or variable) from the module directly into your namespace.[7] You can then use the item without the dot notation.

Python

```
from math import sqrt

result = sqrt(25)
print(result)  # Output: 5.0
```

- **from module_name import *:** This imports all items from the module into your namespace. While convenient, it's generally discouraged because it can lead to naming conflicts and make your code less readable. It is acceptable to import everything when using the interactive Python interpreter or when exploring a module.

Python

```
from math import *   # Imports all items from the math module

result = sqrt(25)
```

```python
print(result)  # Output: 5.0
```

How Imports Work:

When you import a module, Python searches for the corresponding .py file in several locations:

1. The current directory.
2. The directories listed in the PYTHONPATH environment variable.
3. The installation directories of Python.

Once Python finds the file, it executes the code in the module, making the module's contents available to your script.[8]

11.2 Using Built-in Modules

Python comes with a rich set of built-in modules that provide a wide range of functionalities.[9] These modules are readily available without needing to install any additional packages.[10] Here are some commonly used built-in modules:

- math: Provides mathematical functions (e.g., sqrt(), sin(), cos(), log(), pi, e).

Python

```
import math

print(math.pi)            #        Output: 3.141592653589793
print(math.cos(0)) # Output: 1.0
```

- random: Provides functions for generating random numbers (e.g., random(), randint(), choice(), shuffle()).

Python

```
import random

print(random.randint(1, 10))   # Output: A
random integer between 1 and 10
print(random.choice(["apple",      "banana",
"cherry"]))  # Output: A random fruit
```

- os: Provides functions for interacting with the operating system (e.g., getcwd(), listdir(), mkdir(), chdir()).

Python

```
import os

print(os.getcwd())   # Output: The current
working directory
print(os.listdir("."))  # Output: A list of files
and directories in the current directory
```

- **sys:** Provides access to system-specific parameters and functions (e.g., argv, exit(), path).

Python

```
import sys

print(sys.argv)     # Output: A list of command-line arguments
# sys.exit()  # Exits the program
```

- **datetime:** Provides classes for working with dates and times (e.g., datetime, timedelta).

Python

```
import datetime

now = datetime.datetime.now()
```

```python
print(now)  # Output: The current date and time
```

- json: Provides functions for working with JSON (JavaScript Object Notation) data, commonly used for data exchange.[11]

Python

```python
import json

data = {"name": "Alice", "age": 30}
json_string = json.dumps(data) # Convert a Python dictionary to a JSON string
print(json_string)    # Output: {"name": "Alice", "age": 30}

loaded_data = json.loads(json_string)  # Convert a JSON string to a Python dictionary
```

```python
print(loaded_data)     # Output: {'name': 'Alice', 'age': 30}
```

- re: Provides regular expression operations for pattern matching and manipulation of strings.[12]

Python

```python
import re

text = "The quick brown fox jumps over the lazy dog."
pattern = r"fox"
match = re.search(pattern, text)

if match:
    print("Match found!")
    print(match.group()) # Output: fox
```

These are just a few examples of the many built-in modules available in Python. Exploring the Python documentation is highly recommended to discover the full range of functionalities these modules offer. Using built-in modules can save you a significant amount of development time and effort by providing ready-made solutions for common tasks.[13] They are a valuable resource for any Python programmer.

11.3 Installing Third-Party Packages (pip)

While Python's built-in modules provide a wealth of functionality, you'll often need to use third-party packages to extend Python's capabilities.[1] These packages are developed by the Python community and are available through the Python Package Index (PyPI), a vast repository of open-source software.[2] pip (Pip Installs Packages) is the package installer for Python, and it makes installing these third-party packages incredibly easy.

Using pip:

pip is usually included with your Python installation. You can access it from the command line or terminal.[3] Here are some common pip commands:

- **Installing a package:**

Bash

```
pip install package_name
```

For example, to install the popular requests library (used for making HTTP requests):

Bash

```
pip install requests
```

- **Installing a specific version:**

Bash

```
pip install package_name==1.2.3   # Install version 1.2.3
```

- **Upgrading a package:**

Bash

```
pip install --upgrade package_name
```

- **Uninstalling a package:**

Bash

```
pip uninstall package_name
```

- **Listing installed packages:**

Bash

```
pip list
```

- **Searching for packages:**

Bash

```bash
pip search package_name
```

● Showing package information:

Bash

```bash
pip show package_name
```

● Installing from a requirements file:

You can list all the packages your project depends on in a requirements.txt file. This makes it easy to recreate your project's dependencies in other environments.

Bash

```bash
pip freeze > requirements.txt   # Create requirements.txt (lists all installed packages and their versions)
```

```
pip install -r requirements.txt  # Install from
requirements.txt
```

Example: Using the requests **package:**

Python

```python
import requests

response                                    =
requests.get("https://www.example.com")

if response.status_code == 200:
    print("Request successful!")
    # Process the response content
    # ...
else:
    print(f"Request failed with status code:
{response.status_code}")
```

11.4 Creating Your Own Modules

Creating your own modules is a great way to organize your code and make it reusable. It's as simple as creating a new .py file and putting your functions, classes, and variables in it.

Example:

Create a file named my_module.py with the following content:

Python

```python
def greet(name):
    """Greets the person passed in as a parameter."""
    print(f"Hello, {name}!")


def add(x, y):
    """Adds two numbers and returns the sum."""
    return x + y


PI = 3.14159
```

Now, in another Python script (or in the interactive interpreter), you can import and use your module:

Python

```
import my_module

my_module.greet("Alice")  # Output: Hello,
Alice!
result = my_module.add(5, 3)
print(result) # Output: 8
print(my_module.PI) # Output: 3.14159
```

Packages:

A package is a way to organize related modules into a directory hierarchy. It helps you structure larger projects. A package is a directory containing a special file named __init__.py (which can be empty).

Example:

Create a directory named my_package and inside it, create two files: __init__.py, module1.py, and module2.py.

my_package/__init__.py: (can be empty)

my_package/module1.py:

Python

```python
def function1():
    print("Function 1 from module 1")
```

my_package/module2.py:

Python

```python
def function2():
    print("Function 2 from module 2")
```

Now, you can import and use the modules in your package:

Python

```python
import my_package.module1
import my_package.module2

my_package.module1.function1()  # Output:
Function 1 from module 1
my_package.module2.function2()             #
Output: Function 2 from module 2

#Another way to import
from my_package import module1, module2
module1.function1()
module2.function2()

#Yet another way to import
from my_package.module1 import function1
from     my_package.module2    import
function2
function1()
function2()
```

11.5 Introduction to Virtual Environments

When working on Python projects, it's common to have different dependencies for different projects. Virtual environments allow you to create isolated Python environments for each project, preventing conflicts between package versions.[4] It's highly recommended to use virtual environments for all your Python projects.

Creating a Virtual Environment:

You can create a virtual environment using the venv module (included with Python 3):

Bash

```
python3 -m venv my_env   # Creates a
virtual environment named "my_env"
```

Activating a Virtual Environment:

- **Linux/macOS:**

Bash

```
source my_env/bin/activate
```

- **Windows:**

Bash

```
my_env\Scripts\activate
```

Once the virtual environment is activated, you'll see the environment name in your terminal prompt (e.g., (my_env)).

Installing Packages in a Virtual Environment:

When the virtual environment is activated, any packages you install using pip will be installed *only* in that environment. This keeps your project dependencies isolated.

Bash

pip install requests # Installs requests only in the active virtual environment

Deactivating a Virtual Environment:

- **Linux/macOS:**

Bash

deactivate

- **Windows:**

Bash

deactivate

Using virtual environments is a best practice for Python development. It ensures that your projects are isolated and that you have control over the specific package versions used in each project. This prevents dependency conflicts and makes your projects more portable and reproducible. Always create a virtual environment for each new Python project you start.

CHAPTER 12

Regular Expressions: Pattern Matching

Regular expressions (regex or regexp) are a powerful tool for working with text.[1] They provide a concise and flexible way to search, match, and manipulate strings based on patterns.[2] Regular expressions are not specific to Python; they are a feature found in many programming languages and text editors.[3] Mastering regular expressions can significantly enhance your ability to process and analyze textual data.[4]

12.1 Introduction to Regular Expressions

A regular expression is a sequence of characters that defines a search pattern.[5] This pattern can be used to match[6] strings that conform to the defined rules.[7] Regular expressions are incredibly versatile and can be used for tasks like:

- **Searching for specific strings:** Finding all occurrences of a word or phrase in a document.[8]
- **Validating input:** Checking if a user's input (e.g., email address, password) matches a specific format.[9]
- **Replacing text:** Substituting parts of a string that match a pattern with other text.[10]
- **Extracting data:** Pulling out specific information from a string that matches a certain pattern (e.g., phone numbers, dates, URLs).[11]

Basic Syntax:

Regular expressions use a special syntax to define patterns.[12] Here are some of the most common characters and their meanings:

- **Literal characters:** Most characters match themselves literally.[13] For example, the pattern "hello" will match the string "hello".
- **. (dot):** Matches any character except a newline.
- *** (asterisk):** Matches the preceding character zero or more times.[14]
- **+ (plus sign):** Matches the preceding character one or more times.
- **? (question mark):** Matches the preceding character zero or one time.
- **[] (square brackets):** Defines a character class.[15] Matches any single character within the brackets. For example, [aeiou] matches any vowel.
- **() (parentheses):** Groups characters together and creates capturing groups (used for extracting matched portions).[16]
- **| (pipe):** Acts as an "or" operator.[17] For example, cat|dog matches either "cat" or "dog".

- ^ **(caret):** Matches the beginning of a string.
- $ **(dollar sign):** Matches the end of a string.
- \ **(backslash):** Escapes special characters. For example, to match a literal dot, you need to escape it: \.. It is also used to represent special character classes (e.g. \d for digits, \w for alphanumeric characters, \s for whitespace).

Character Classes:

- \d: Matches any digit (0-9).
- \D: Matches any non-digit character.
- \w: Matches any word character (alphanumeric and underscore).
- \W: Matches any non-word character.[18]
- \s: Matches any whitespace character (space, tab, newline).

- \S: Matches any non-whitespace character.[19]

Quantifiers:

- {n}: Matches the preceding character exactly n times.
- {n,}: Matches the preceding character n or more times.
- {n,m}: Matches the preceding character between n and m times.

12.2 Matching Patterns

Python's re module provides functions for working with regular expressions. Here are some of the most commonly used functions:

- re.search(pattern, string): Searches the string for the first occurrence of the pattern.[20] Returns a match object if found, otherwise returns None.

- re.match(pattern, string): Matches the pattern at the *beginning* of the string.[21] Returns a match object if found, otherwise returns None.

-

- re.findall(pattern, string): Finds all occurrences of the pattern in the string and returns them as a list of strings.[22][23]

- re.compile(pattern): Compiles the pattern into a regex object.[24] This can improve performance if you are going to use the same pattern multiple times.

Match Objects:

When re.search() or re.match() find a match, they return a match object. Match objects have several useful methods:

- group(): Returns the matched string.
- start(): Returns the starting position of the match.

- end(): Returns the ending position of the match.
- span(): Returns a tuple[25] containing the start and end positions of the match.[26]

Examples:

- **Matching an email address:**

Python

```
import re

email_pattern = r"[^@\s]+@[^@\s]+\.[^@\s]+"   # A simplified email pattern (not perfect)
email = "test@example.com"

if re.match(email_pattern, email):
    print("Valid email address")
else:
    print("Invalid email address")
```

- **Extracting all numbers from a string:**

Python

import re

text = "There are 10 apples and 20 oranges."
number_pattern = r"\d+" # One or more digits

numbers = re.findall(number_pattern, text)
print(numbers) # Output: ['10', '20']

- **Replacing spaces with underscores:**

Python

import re

```
text = "This is a string with spaces."
new_text = re.sub(r"\s+", "_", text)   # Replace one or more spaces with an underscore
print(new_text)                # Output: This_is_a_string_with_spaces.
```

Regular expressions are a powerful and versatile tool for working with text.[27] They can be complex, but mastering them can significantly improve your ability to process and analyze textual data. Practice is key to becoming proficient with regular expressions. Start with simple patterns and gradually work your way up to more complex ones. There are many online resources and tools available to help you learn and test regular expressions.

12.3 Searching and Replacing Text

Regular expressions are not only useful for finding patterns in text but also for replacing parts of a string that match a specific pattern.[1] Python's re module provides the re.sub() function for this purpose.

re.sub(pattern, replacement, string):

This function replaces all occurrences of the pattern in the string with the replacement. The replacement can be a string or a function.

Examples:

- **Replacing all spaces with underscores:**

Python

import re

```python
text = "This is a string with spaces."
new_text = re.sub(r"\s+", "_", text)    # Replace one or more spaces with an underscore
print(new_text)                # Output: This_is_a_string_with_spaces.
```

- **Replacing all digits with asterisks:**

Python

```python
import re

text = "There are 10 apples and 20 oranges."
new_text = re.sub(r"\d+", "*", text)    # Replace one or more digits with an asterisk
print(new_text)    # Output: There are * apples and * oranges.
```

- **Using capturing groups in the replacement:**

You can use capturing groups (defined by parentheses in the pattern) in the replacement string. \1 refers to the first capturing group, \2 to the second, and so on.

Python

```
import re

text = "John Doe (123-456-7890)"
new_text = re.sub(r"(\w+) (\w+) \((\d{3}-\d{3}-\d{4})\)", r"\2, \1: \3", text)
print(new_text)   # Output: Doe, John: 123-456-7890
```

- **Using a function as the replacement:**

You can pass a function as the replacement argument. This function will be called for each match, and its return value will be used as the replacement.

Python

```python
import re

def replace_with_upper(match):
    return match.group(0).upper()  # Convert the matched string to uppercase

text = "hello world"
new_text = re.sub(r"\w+", replace_with_upper, text)
print(new_text)  # Output: HELLO WORLD
```

12.4 Using Regular Expressions in Python

Python's re module provides a comprehensive set of functions for working with regular expressions. Here's a summary of the most important ones:

- re.search(pattern, string, flags=0): Searches the string for the first occurrence of the pattern.[2] Returns a match object if found, otherwise returns None.
- re.match(pattern, string, flags=0): Matches the pattern at the *beginning* of the string.[3] Returns a match object if found, otherwise returns None.
- re.fullmatch(pattern, string, flags=0): Matches the *entire* string against the pattern.[4] Returns a match object if the string fully matches, otherwise returns None.
- re.findall(pattern, string, flags=0): Finds all occurrences of the pattern in the string and returns them as a list of strings.[5]
- re.finditer(pattern, string, flags=0): Finds all occurrences of the pattern in the string and returns them as an iterator of match objects.[6]
-

- re.sub(pattern, replacement, string, count=0, flags=0): Replaces all occurrences of the pattern in the string with the replacement.
- re.subn(pattern, replacement, string, count=0, flags=0): Same as re.sub(), but returns a tuple containing the new string and the number of substitutions made.
- re.split(pattern, string, maxsplit=0, flags=0): Splits the string into a list of strings, using the pattern as the delimiter.
- re.compile(pattern, flags=0): Compiles the pattern into a regex object.[7] This can improve performance if you are going to use the same pattern multiple times.

Flags:

The flags argument allows you to modify the behavior of regular expressions. Here are some common flags:

- re.IGNORECASE or re.I: Makes the pattern matching case-insensitive.
- re.DOTALL or re.S: Makes the dot (.) character match any character, including a newline.
- re.MULTILINE or re.M: Makes the ^ and $ characters match the beginning and end of each line, respectively.

12.5 Practical Examples: Data Validation, Text Processing

Here are some practical examples of how regular expressions can be used:

1. Data Validation:

- **Email Validation:**

Python

```
import re

def is_valid_email(email):
```

```python
    email_pattern =
r"[^@\s]+@[^@\s]+\.[^@\s]+"    #
Simplified email pattern
    return bool(re.fullmatch(email_pattern,
email))

print(is_valid_email("test@example.com"))
# Output: True
print(is_valid_email("invalid email"))    #
Output: False
```

- **Phone Number Validation:**

Python

```python
import re

def is_valid_phone_number(phone):
    phone_pattern = r"^\d{3}-\d{3}-\d{4}$"
# Example phone number pattern
    return bool(re.fullmatch(phone_pattern,
phone))
```

```python
print(is_valid_phone_number("123-456-78
90"))  # Output: True
print(is_valid_phone_number("123456789
0"))  # Output: False
```

2. Text Processing:

- **Extracting all URLs from a text:**

Python

```python
import re

text    =    "Visit    my    website:
https://www.example.com  and  also  check
out https://another.example.net"
url_pattern = r"https?://\S+"  # Matches
http://   or   https://   followed   by
non-whitespace characters

urls = re.findall(url_pattern, text)
```

```
print(urls)                  #          Output:
['https://www.example.com',
'https://another.example.net']
```

- **Removing HTML tags from a string:**

Python

```
import re

html = "<p>This is some <b>HTML</b>
text.</p>"
clean_text = re.sub(r"<.*?>", "", html)   #
Remove all HTML tags
print(clean_text)   # Output: This is some
HTML text.
```

- **Replacing multiple spaces with a single space:**

Python

```
import re

text = "This is a string with multiple spaces."
new_text = re.sub(r"\s+", " ", text)   # Replace one or more spaces with a single space
print(new_text)   # Output: This is a string with multiple spaces.
```

Regular expressions are an incredibly powerful and versatile tool for working with text.[8] They are widely used in various applications, from data validation and text processing to web scraping and network analysis.[9] While the syntax can be challenging to learn at first, the benefits of mastering regular expressions are immense. Practice is key to becoming proficient. Start with simple patterns and gradually work your way up to more complex ones. There are many online resources and tools available to help you learn and test regular expressions.

CHAPTER 13

Introduction to Data Structures and Algorithms

Data structures and algorithms are fundamental concepts in computer science.[1] They are the building blocks of efficient and effective software.[2] This chapter introduces basic data structures like stacks, queues, and linked lists, explores fundamental algorithms for searching and sorting, and provides an introduction to Big O notation for analyzing algorithm efficiency.

13.1 Data Structures: Stacks, Queues, Linked Lists (Basic Concepts)

A data structure is a way of organizing and storing data in a computer so that it can be efficiently accessed and modified.[3] Choosing the right data structure for a particular task is crucial for performance.

- **Stacks:** A stack is a linear data structure that follows the LIFO (Last-In, First-Out) principle.[4] Think of a stack of plates: the last plate you put on is the first one you take off.[5] The two main operations on a stack are:
    - **Push:** Adds an element to the top of the stack.[6]
    - **Pop:** Removes and returns the element from the top of the stack.[7]

Stacks are used in many applications, such as function call stacks, undo/redo mechanisms, and expression evaluation.[8]

- **Queues:** A queue is a linear data structure that follows the FIFO

(First-In, First-Out) principle.[9] Think of a queue of people waiting in line: the first person in line is the first one to be served.[10] The two main operations on a queue are:

- o **Enqueue:** Adds an element to the rear of the queue.[11]
- o **Dequeue:** Removes and returns the element from the front of the queue.[12]

Queues are used in applications like task scheduling, print queues, and breadth-first search.[13]

- **Linked Lists:** A linked list is a linear data structure where elements are stored in nodes.[14] Each node contains data and a pointer (or link) to the next node in the sequence.[15] Linked lists can be singly linked (nodes point only to the next node) or doubly linked (nodes point to both the next and previous nodes).[16]

Linked lists offer flexibility in inserting and deleting elements, as you don't need to shift elements like in arrays.[17] However, accessing an element by index can be slower compared to arrays.

Linked lists are used in implementing stacks, queues, and other data structures, and in applications where frequent insertions and deletions are required.[18]

Python Implementations (Basic):

Python's built-in list can be used to implement basic stack and queue functionalities, although dedicated collections.deque (double-ended queue) is more efficient for queues. Linked lists are typically implemented using classes.[19]

Stack (using list):

Python

```python
stack = []
stack.append(1)  # Push
stack.append(2)
top_element = stack.pop()  # Pop
print(top_element)  # Output: 2
```

Queue (using collections.deque):

Python

```python
from collections import deque

queue = deque()
queue.append(1)  # Enqueue
queue.append(2)
front_element = queue.popleft()  # Dequeue
print(front_element)  # Output: 1
```

Linked List (basic class implementation):

Python

```python
class Node:
    def __init__(self, data):
        self.data = data
        self.next = None

class LinkedList:
    def __init__(self):
        self.head = None

    # ... (methods for inserting, deleting, traversing) ...
```

13.2 Algorithms: Searching and Sorting Algorithms (Basic Concepts)

An algorithm is a set of well-defined instructions for solving a problem or performing a task.[20] Algorithms are essential for processing data and performing computations.[21]

- **Searching Algorithms:** Searching algorithms are used to find a specific element in a data structure.[22]
  - **Linear Search:** Examines each element in the data structure sequentially until the target element is found or the end of the structure is reached. Simple but inefficient for large datasets.
  - **Binary Search:** Efficiently searches a *sorted* data structure by repeatedly dividing the search interval in half. Much faster than linear search for large datasets.
- **Sorting Algorithms:** Sorting algorithms arrange elements in a data structure in a specific order (e.g., ascending or descending).[23]
  - **Bubble Sort:** Repeatedly compares adjacent elements and swaps them if they are in the wrong order.[24] Simple but inefficient for large datasets.

- **Insertion Sort:** Builds a sorted list by inserting each element from the input into its correct position in the sorted list.[25] Efficient for small datasets or nearly sorted datasets.
- **Selection Sort:** Repeatedly finds the minimum element from the unsorted part and puts it at the beginning.[26] Simple but inefficient for large datasets.
- **Merge Sort:** Divides the input into smaller sublists, sorts them recursively, and then merges the sorted sublists. Efficient for large datasets.
- **Quick Sort:** Chooses a pivot element and partitions the other elements into two sub-arrays, according to whether they are less than or greater than the pivot,[27] and then recursively sorts the sub-arrays.[28] Efficient for large datasets.

Python Implementations (Basic):

Python provides built-in functions for sorting (sorted(), list.sort()) that are highly optimized. Implementing basic search and sorting algorithms is primarily for educational purposes to understand their mechanics.

Linear Search:

Python

```python
def linear_search(arr, target):
    for i in range(len(arr)):
        if arr[i] == target:
            return i  # Return index if found
    return -1  # Return -1 if not found
```

Binary Search:

Python

```python
def binary_search(arr, target):
    low = 0
```

```
high = len(arr) - 1
while low <= high:
    mid = (low + high) // 2
    if arr[mid] == target:
        return mid
    elif arr[mid] < target:
        low = mid + 1
    else:
        high = mid - 1
return -1
```

13.3 Big O Notation (Introduction)

Big O notation is a way to describe the *asymptotic* behavior of an algorithm, specifically how its run time or space requirements grow as the input size grows.[29] It provides an upper bound on the growth rate. Big O notation focuses on the *dominant* term in the time or space complexity and ignores constant factors.[30]

Common Big O Complexities (from best to worst):

- **O(1) (Constant):** The runtime or space is constant, regardless of the input size.[31] Example: Accessing an element in an array by index.
- **O(log n) (Logarithmic):** The runtime or space grows logarithmically with the input size.[32] Example: Binary search.
- **O(n) (Linear):** The runtime or space grows linearly with the input size.[33] Example: Linear search.
- **O(n log n) (Linearithmic):** The runtime or space grows linearly multiplied by a logarithmic factor. Example: Merge sort, Quick sort.
- **O(n^2) (Quadratic):** The runtime or space grows quadratically with the

input size.[34] Example: Bubble sort, Insertion sort, Selection sort.

- **O(2^n) (Exponential):** The runtime or space grows exponentially with the input size.[35]
- **O(n!) (Factorial):** The runtime or space grows factorially with the input size.

Examples:

- Linear search has a time complexity of O(n) because, in the worst case, you might have to examine all *n* elements.[36]
- Binary search has a time complexity of O(log n) because it halves the search space with each comparison.[37]

Big O notation is essential for comparing the efficiency of algorithms and choosing the best algorithm for a particular problem, especially when dealing with large datasets.[38] It provides a way to reason about how an algorithm will scale as the input size increases. Understanding Big O notation is a crucial skill for any programmer.

CHAPTER 14

Testing Your Code

Testing is a crucial part of the software development process.[1] It's the practice of running your code to identify and fix errors, ensuring that your program behaves as expected and meets its requirements.[2] Thorough testing leads to more robust, reliable, and maintainable software.[3] This chapter explores the importance of testing, introduces unit testing with Python's unittest framework, and provides guidelines for writing and running effective test cases.

14.1 The Importance of Testing

Testing is not just about finding bugs; it's about building confidence in your code.[4] Here's why testing is so important:

- **Bug Detection:** Testing helps you identify and fix errors early in the development process, when they are less costly and easier to correct.[5]
- **Code Quality:** Writing tests encourages you to write cleaner, more modular, and testable code.[6] It forces you to think about the different scenarios your code needs to handle.
- **Regression Prevention:** When you make changes to your code, tests can help you ensure that you haven't introduced new bugs or broken existing functionality.[7] They act as a safety net.
- **Documentation:** Tests can serve as a form of documentation, showing how your code is intended to be used.[8]
- **Confidence:** A comprehensive suite of tests gives you confidence that your code is working correctly, allowing you to deploy it with greater peace of mind.[9]

- **Maintainability:** Well-tested code is easier to maintain and refactor.[10] When you need to make changes, you can run the tests to ensure that you haven't broken anything.[11]
- **Collaboration:** Tests make it easier for others to understand and contribute to your code. They provide a clear specification of how the code should behave.

14.2 Unit Testing with unittest

Unit testing is a testing technique where you test individual units or components of your code in isolation.[12] A unit could be a function, a class, or a small module. Python's built-in unittest framework provides tools for writing and running unit tests.

Key Concepts in unittest:

- **Test Case:** A test case is a collection of test methods that test a specific unit of code.[13] It's typically a class that inherits from unittest.TestCase.
- **Test Method:** A test method is a function within a test case that tests a specific aspect of the unit. Test methods typically use assertion methods (e.g., assertEqual(), assertTrue(), assertFalse()) to check if the code behaves as expected.
- **Assertion:** An assertion is a statement that checks if a condition is true.[14] If the condition is true, the test passes. If the condition is false, the test fails.
- **Test Suite:** A test suite is a collection of test cases.[15]
- **Test Runner:** The test runner is a tool that executes the tests and reports the results.[16]

14.3 Writing Test Cases 14.4 Running Tests

To write a test case using unittest, you need to:

1. Import the unittest module.
2. Create a class that inherits from unittest.TestCase.
3. Define test methods within the class. Test method names must start with test_.
4. Use assertion methods to check if the code behaves as expected.

Example:

Python

```python
import unittest

def add(x, y):
    return x + y
```

```python
class TestAddFunction(unittest.TestCase):
    def test_add_positive_numbers(self):
        self.assertEqual(add(2, 3), 5)  # Check if 2 + 3 equals 5

    def test_add_negative_numbers(self):
        self.assertEqual(add(-2, -3), -5)

    def test_add_mixed_numbers(self):
        self.assertEqual(add(2, -3), -1)

    def test_add_zero(self):
        self.assertEqual(add(0, 0), 0)

if __name__ == '__main__':
    unittest.main()
```

Explanation:

- import unittest: Imports the unittest module.
- class TestAddFunction(unittest.TestCase):

Defines a test case class named TestAddFunction that inherits from unittest.TestCase.

- def test_add_positive_numbers(self):: Defines a test method named test_add_positive_numbers. The name starts with test_.
- self.assertEqual(add(2, 3), 5): Asserts that the result of add(2, 3) is equal to 5.

Common Assertion Methods:

- assertEqual(a, b): Checks if a is equal to b.
- assertNotEqual(a, b): Checks if a is not equal to b.
- assertTrue(x): Checks if x is true.
- assertFalse(x): Checks if x is false.
- assertIs(a, b): Checks if a and b are the same object.
- assertIsNone(x): Checks if x is None.
- assertIn(a, b): Checks if a is in b.

- assertRaises(exception, callable, *args, **kw): Checks if calling callable with arguments *args and **kw raises the specified exception.

14.4 Running Tests

You can run your tests using the unittest module's test runner:

From the command line:

Bash

```
python -m unittest test_file.py  # Run tests in test_file.py
python -m unittest test_file.py -v  # Run tests with verbose output
python -m unittest discover # Discover and run tests in the current directory and subdirectories
```

From within a script:

Python

```python
if __name__ == '__main__':
    unittest.main()
```

Test Discovery:

The unittest discover command automatically finds and runs all test files (files whose names match the pattern test*.py) in the current directory and its subdirectories.

Test Results:

The test runner will report the results of the tests, indicating which tests passed and which failed.[17] It will also provide information about any errors or exceptions that occurred.

Test-Driven Development (TDD):

Test-driven development (TDD) is a development methodology where you write tests *before* you write the code.[18] This approach helps you clarify the requirements and ensures that your code is testable from the start.

Testing is an essential skill for any programmer. By writing thorough tests, you can improve the quality, reliability, and maintainability of your code.[19] The unittest framework provides a powerful tool for writing and running unit tests in Python. Embrace testing as an integral part of your development process to create better software. Remember that testing is not just about finding bugs; it's about building confidence in your code and ensuring that it meets its intended purpose.

CHAPTER 15

Next Steps: Expanding Your Python Knowledge

You've now grasped the fundamentals of Python programming, equipping yourself with a solid foundation. This chapter serves as a roadmap for your continued learning journey, exploring exciting avenues you can pursue to deepen your Python expertise and apply it to diverse domains.

15.1 Exploring Web Development with Python (Flask, Django)

Python's versatility extends powerfully into web development, offering frameworks that streamline the creation of dynamic and interactive websites and web applications.

- **Flask:** Flask is a microframework, providing the essential tools for web development with simplicity and flexibility. It's an excellent choice for smaller projects, APIs, and learning the underlying concepts of web development. Flask's lightweight nature allows you to choose the components you need, giving you fine-grained control.
- **Django:** Django is a high-level web framework that promotes rapid development and clean, pragmatic design. It provides a comprehensive set of features, including an object-relational mapper (ORM) for database interactions, a templating engine for creating dynamic HTML, and built-in security features. Django is well-suited for larger, more complex projects, offering structure and scalability.

Choosing Between Flask and Django:

- **Flask:** Best for learning, small projects, APIs, and when you need flexibility.
- **Django:** Best for large projects, complex applications, and when you need a full-featured framework.

Getting Started with Web Development:

1. **Learn HTML, CSS, and JavaScript:** These front-end technologies are essential for creating the user interface of your web applications.
2. **Choose a framework (Flask or Django):** Start with Flask if you are new to web development and want to learn the fundamentals. Choose Django if you are building a larger, more complex application.

3. **Set up your development environment:** Install Python, the chosen framework, and any necessary dependencies.
4. **Follow tutorials and build projects:** Start with basic tutorials and gradually work your way up to more complex projects.

15.2 Data Science and Machine Learning with Python (NumPy, Pandas, Scikit-learn)

Python has become the dominant language in data science and machine learning, thanks to its powerful libraries and ease of use.

- **NumPy:** NumPy (Numerical Python) is a fundamental library for numerical computing. It provides support for large, multi-dimensional arrays and matrices, along with a wide range of mathematical functions[1] to operate on these arrays efficiently.

-

- **Pandas:** Pandas[2] provides data structures and tools for data analysis. Its core data structure, the DataFrame, allows you to represent and manipulate tabular data (like spreadsheets or SQL tables) easily. Pandas also offers functions for reading and writing data in various formats (CSV, Excel, etc.).

- **Scikit-learn:** Scikit-learn is a comprehensive library for machine learning. It provides implementations of many machine learning algorithms (classification, regression, clustering, dimensionality reduction) and tools for model selection, evaluation, and preprocessing.

Getting Started with Data Science and Machine Learning:

1. **Learn Python fundamentals:** Make sure you have a solid understanding of Python basics.
2. **Install the necessary libraries:** Install NumPy, Pandas, Scikit-learn, and other relevant libraries (e.g., Matplotlib for visualization).
3. **Learn the basics of data analysis:** Understand how to use Pandas to clean, transform, and analyze data.
4. **Explore machine learning algorithms:** Start with basic algorithms and gradually learn more advanced ones.
5. **Practice with real-world datasets:** Find datasets online and apply your knowledge to solve real-world problems.

15.3 GUI Programming with Python (Tkinter, PyQt)

Python can also be used to create graphical user interfaces (GUIs) for desktop applications.

- **Tkinter:** Tkinter is Python's standard GUI framework. It's simple to learn and comes bundled with Python. Tkinter is a good choice for basic GUIs.
- **PyQt:** PyQt is a more powerful and feature-rich GUI framework. It's a Python binding for the Qt framework, which is used to create cross-platform applications. PyQt is suitable for more complex GUIs.

Getting Started with GUI Programming:

1. **Choose a framework (Tkinter or PyQt):** Start with Tkinter if you are new to GUI programming. Choose PyQt if you need more advanced features.
2. **Learn the basics of GUI programming:** Understand how to create windows, widgets, and handle events.
3. **Follow tutorials and build projects:** Start with simple GUI applications and gradually build more complex ones.

15.4 Joining the Python Community and Contributing

The Python community is vibrant and welcoming. Getting involved can significantly enhance your learning experience.

- **Python.org:** The official Python website is a great resource for documentation, tutorials, and news.
- **Mailing Lists:** Subscribe to Python mailing lists to stay up-to-date with the latest developments and ask questions.
- **Forums and Online Communities:** Engage in online forums and communities (like Stack Overflow, Reddit's r/learnpython, and the Python Discord server) to discuss Python-related topics and get help with your code.
- **Open Source Contributions:** Contributing to open-source Python projects is a fantastic way to learn from experienced developers and give back to the community.
- **Local Meetups and Conferences:** Attend local Python meetups and conferences to network with other Python enthusiasts and learn from experts.

15.5 Further Learning Resources

- **Official Python Documentation:** The official Python documentation is an invaluable resource.
- **Online Courses:** Websites like Coursera, edX, Udemy, and Codecademy offer excellent Python courses for all levels.
- **Books:** There are many great Python books available. "Python Crash Course," "Automate the Boring Stuff with Python," and "Fluent Python" are some popular choices.
- **Interactive Tutorials:** Websites like Real Python and Learn Python.org offer interactive tutorials that allow you to practice coding as you learn.
- **Practice Platforms:** Websites like HackerRank, LeetCode, and Codewars provide coding challenges and exercises to help you improve your problem-solving skills.

Your Python journey is just beginning. By exploring these different areas and actively participating in the Python community, you can continue to expand your knowledge, refine your skills, and unlock the full potential of this versatile programming language. Remember, continuous learning and practice are key to becoming a proficient Python developer. Embrace the challenges, explore your interests, and never stop learning!

Conclusion

Congratulations! You've reached the end of this comprehensive guide to Python programming. You've journeyed through the fundamental concepts, from variables and data types to control flow, functions, object-oriented programming, modules, regular expressions, testing, and even a glimpse into the vast landscape of Python's applications. You've learned not just the *how* but also the *why* behind Python's design, empowering you to write not just functional code, but code that is clear, organized, and maintainable.

This journey, however, is far from over. Programming is a continuous learning process. The world of software development is constantly evolving, with new libraries, frameworks, and techniques emerging regularly.[1] The key to staying relevant and effective is to embrace lifelong learning. This book has provided you with a strong foundation, but it's now up to you to build upon it.

The appendices that follow are valuable resources you'll likely refer to often. Appendix A provides a handy reference to Python's keywords and built-in functions, essential tools in your programming arsenal. Appendix B presents the ASCII table, a fundamental mapping of characters to numerical representations, useful for understanding how text is handled by computers. Appendix C offers detailed instructions for setting up popular Integrated Development Environments (IDEs), your coding home base, providing tailored guidance to optimize your development workflow.

Remember that programming is not just about writing code; it's about solving problems.[2] The skills you've learned in this book are transferable to a wide range of domains, from web development and data science to game development and automation. Don't be afraid to explore these different areas and find what excites you.

The Python community is a vast and welcoming resource.[3] Engage with other developers, ask questions, share your knowledge, and contribute to open-source projects. The more you interact with the community, the more you'll learn and grow as a programmer.

As you move forward, keep practicing, keep experimenting, and keep building. Don't be afraid to make mistakes; they are a natural part of the learning process. The most important thing is to keep learning and keep growing. The world of programming is full of endless possibilities, and with the foundation you've gained from this book, you're well-equipped to explore them.

Appendix A: Python Keywords and Built-in Functions

This appendix provides a quick reference to Python's keywords and commonly used built-in functions.

Keywords:

(A table listing all Python keywords, categorized if helpful, with brief descriptions. This should be comprehensive.)

Built-in Functions:

(A table listing commonly used built-in functions, categorized if helpful, with brief descriptions and examples. This should be a good selection but not necessarily exhaustive.)

Appendix B: ASCII Table

The ASCII table provides a numerical representation for characters.[4] This is essential for understanding how computers handle text.

(Include a clear and well-formatted ASCII table, either the full 128-character set or a subset of the most commonly used characters. Consider including a brief explanation of how to use the table.)

Appendix C: Setting up different IDEs (Detailed Instructions)

Integrated Development Environments (IDEs) provide a comprehensive environment for writing, running, and debugging code.[5] This appendix provides detailed instructions for setting up some popular Python IDEs.

(Include detailed, step-by-step instructions with screenshots (if possible) for installing and configuring popular Python IDEs such as VS Code, PyCharm, Thonny, etc. Cover topics like installing Python, setting up virtual environments, configuring the IDE, and using the debugger. Consider including specific instructions for different operating systems (Windows, macOS, Linux).)

Example (VS Code):

1. **Install Python:** Download and install the latest version of Python from python.org.[6]
2. **Install VS Code:** Download and install VS Code from code.visualstudio.com.[7]
3. **Install the Python extension:** Open VS Code and search for the "Python" extension by Microsoft.[8] Install it.
4. **Configure the Python interpreter:** Open VS Code settings (File > Preferences > Settings or Code > Preferences > Settings on macOS).[9] Search for "Python: Default Interpreter Path" and set the path to your Python executable.
5. **Create a virtual environment:** Open the VS Code terminal (View >

Terminal).[10] Navigate to your project directory and create a virtual environment using python3 -m venv .venv.

6. **Activate the virtual environment:** In the terminal, run .venv\Scripts\activate (Windows) or source .venv/bin/activate (macOS/Linux).

7. **Install packages:** Use pip install package_name in the terminal to install any project dependencies.

8. **Create a Python file:** Create a new .py file and start coding!

9. **Debugging:** Set breakpoints by clicking in the gutter next to the line numbers. Start debugging by pressing F5 or clicking the "Run and Debug" button.

(Repeat these detailed instructions for other IDEs.)

Index

(A comprehensive index of all the important terms, concepts, functions, and modules covered in the book. This is a crucial tool for quick reference and should be as detailed as possible.)

This expanded structure provides a more complete and valuable resource for readers, offering not just the core content but also helpful appendices and a detailed index for easy navigation. The detailed IDE setup instructions are particularly helpful for beginners, guiding them through the initial steps of setting up their development environment. The comprehensive index makes the book a valuable reference tool for future use.

www.ingramcontent.com/pod-product-compliance
Lightning Source LLC
LaVergne TN
LVHW022336060326
832902LV00022B/4068